Books written previously by the same author:

'Our Birth on Earth'

'When Scorpio Ruled the World'

'Heaven's Message – How to Read it Nowadays'

'Character Portraits of England's Plantagenet Kings'

'Concise Character Portraits of England's Tudor, Stuart and Protectorate Rulers'

'Character Portraits of England's Germanic Monarchs'

Simply
Now

Our Simple,
AD 2020 Situation

Chris Stubbs

Order this book online at www.trafford.com
or email orders@trafford.com

Most Trafford titles are also available at major online book retailers.

© Copyright 2016 Chris Stubbs.
All rights reserved. No part of this publication may be reproduced, stored in a retrieval system, or transmitted, in any form or by any means, electronic, mechanical, photocopying, recording, or otherwise, without the written prior permission of the author.

Print information available on the last page.

ISBN: 978-1-4907-7885-3 (sc)
ISBN: 978-1-4907-7886-0 (e)

Library of Congress Control Number: 2016920035

Because of the dynamic nature of the Internet, any web addresses or links contained in this book may have changed since publication and may no longer be valid. The views expressed in this work are solely those of the author and do not necessarily reflect the views of the publisher, and the publisher hereby disclaims any responsibility for them.

Any people depicted in stock imagery provided by Thinkstock are models, and such images are being used for illustrative purposes only.
Certain stock imagery © Thinkstock.

Trafford rev. 12/08/2016

www.trafford.com
North America & international
toll-free: 1 888 232 4444 (USA & Canada)
fax: 812 355 4082

To the memory of William MacNeile Dixon (1866 – 1946)
Gifford Lecturer, Glasgow University.

ACKNOWLEDGEMENTS

Once again, Lois Rodden's website: 'Astro.com' proved useful as a source of rated birth data. Additionally, the staff of Wirral Libraries, Bromborough Branch, kindly obtained for me, books that were difficult to come by. My wife, Angela, made time available for writing the book.

CONTENTS

FOREWORD

This book is the last in a series of seven books. All of the previous six have been leading up to this final one. Recently, Cox and Cohen have published a praiseworthy series of 'Wonders' books of recent science, and Harari has produced a fascinating book on a 'History of Humankind'. But there appeared to be two gaps between them that could be filled by the supportive cases of 'Life Chemistry' and of 'Personality'. Because humans are far better at making comparisons, rather than at making direct objective assessments, chapters 1 and 2 present a rearranged précis of 'The Human Situation' by W. MacNeile Dixon, published in 1937. The contents of these two chapters seem remarkably relevant to our situation today. Chapter 3 tells us what we are not going to talk about, what we are going to talk about and then introduces 'Life Chemistry' that comprises a large part of Organic Chemistry, i.e. the chemistry of carbon. Now chapter 2 predicts that individual personalities will become more important as society develops in the future. Accordingly, chapter 4 deals with the origin of our personalities, how we can describe them and how far we have come in trying to prove how valid these descriptions are. Chapter 5 shows how personality descriptions can be produced and then suggests uses to which they can be put. Finally, chapter 6 addresses various points from chapters 1 and 2 as they appear to us today, as well as answering several questions raised there. Chapter 6 ends by indicating how we should proceed collectively, into our long-term future.

- -

CHAPTER 1

OUR SIMPLE 1940 A.D. SITUATION

Abstracted and rearranged from 'The Human Situation' by W. MacNeile Dixon.

Part 1 – both material and immaterial.

Let us begin with ourselves. We are alive, are aware of our surroundings and have characters to enjoy, or to grieve over our condition. The Sun rises and sets, the tides rise and fall and people eat, drink and take their pleasures regardless, as if nothing is happening. Yet the first and fundamental wonder is existence itself. That 'I' should have emerged out of nothingness, that the Void should have given birth not merely to things but to 'me', a conscious, live person, is astonishing. During our early years, when all was fresh and new, we took the miracle for granted. We were busy becoming accustomed to living, and nothing of this appeared startling. We accepted life without even asking, "Why should there be anything at all?" But let our minds once awake and this emergence from the womb of the immeasurable Universe rises to its full significance. To find oneself a member of a particular society, with all its own multitudinous affairs, and not knowing why this should be, and how we came into possession of our own particular characters, provokes numerous philosophical questions leading one to become a member of a very negligible minority. Few humans have become concerned with such musings. Most have died, whatever their pursuits, in the vigour of their sensuality and in the full stride of their ignorance. If there has been one God acknowledged universally and worshipped throughout all ages and countries; it is money.

All forms of life, all organisms that have been made manifest, are engaged in an unceasing struggle to maintain themselves against the forces of nature. "To live, my dear Lucullus, is to make war." Each of us, is born with no reasons given, as a man or a woman, an Arab, an Andaman islander, a Chinese coolie, an English gentleman, a St. Thomas, or an Ivan the Terrible. Each is born in the Stone Age, the fifth or fifteenth century, a vegetarian, cannibal, of base or noble stock, the child of half-witted parents, an imbecile, or a fanatic. As an accident of birth, each of us inherits a family blood feud, a belief in Voodoo, or in a Christian creed of love and charity, and so on. Is it accidental, or is it a selection made by each one of us in a previous state? And what is the justice, if one of us languishes on a bed of sickness, while another enjoys health and happiness? These inequalities of place, time, heredity and circumstance are strewn among us with a monstrous partiality. Under what conditions are we allotted good looks, a musical ear, a sunny temper, a talent for figures, or denied these qualities? And from these bodies of ours there is no escape. They do as much as they please with us. What a despot is the stomach! We can be nauseated by ourselves, or nervously and shamefacedly avert our eyes from the dishonours we must endure.

Good health too, has always been prized as the first and greatest of blessings. Yet perfect health is not common. That bad health lies at the root of a great proportion of human suffering and misery, is beyond dispute. A legion of ills spring from this cause, ranging from bad temper to theft and from drugs and drunkenness to suicide and murder. Health is the high road to Earthly happiness. Both health and illness are, in part, a matter of inheritance, yet hardly, if at all less, a matter of climate. The tropics induce inertia and enfeeble purpose, while in too stimulating climates, the struggle to keep alive is exhausting. Possibly, the British Isles enjoy the healthiest climate in which mankind is at its best, both physically and intellectually. As for the British, "Time, the ocean and some favouring star, in high cabal, have made us what we are."

We may also ask whether we have been created by a nature with no interest in man. Men are simply animals, one species among many thousands. Lords of creation maybe, but certainly not heirs of heaven. Viewed from the dimensions of space, no comparisons can better express the insignificance of man among the cosmic magnitudes. In a Universe so wide, how can we creatures of a day strut, pose and bluster, or look upon ourselves without contempt? Also, how slight a thing is man, even amid the works of man himself. The pyramids belittle the pharaohs who built them. Caesar in his capital of Rome, the archbishop beneath his cathedral's soaring towers and the captain on the bridge of his battleship, are barely visible among their magnificent surroundings, and so present but a poor appearance.

However, we should not accept the philosophy, either of the telescope, or the microscope – to be overpowered by mere magnitude is preposterous. This material perspective is the most distorting and cheapest of our many illusions, overlooking the mind that knows more about the stars than they ever will know themselves until their dying day. But man is at once contained within, and yet himself contains, the World in his thought. Thus, if his outer and physical visions minimise his importance, his inner and intellectual ones restore and enhance it.

Let us turn now to the surrounding World. When life appeared, it did so in a World that somehow supported it. Life depends upon nutrition, and cannot get along using only its own resources. Somehow the World supports us and we are nourished in both body and mind. Also, on its arrival upon the scene, the living creature anticipates that it will receive the necessary assistance. The baby is extremely annoyed if its food is not forthcoming. Nor, despite this tremendous assumption, is it usually disappointed. Animals, the moment that they are born, are already experts in their several ways of life. These strange circumstances suggest a harmony between living things and their surroundings. The World is just as suited to be the home of living things, as they are to make it their home. Certainly, there are some remarkable features of our planet that suggest that it was designed as a grand theatre, as if the coming and conduct of life had been anticipated somehow. Had things been otherwise, we should not have been here to discuss them. At first sight, the conditions looked far from promising. But there were notable peculiarities in the situation. For example, the greatest density of water occurs at a temperature of 4^0C, so that when ice forms, it floats on the remaining water in order that life can continue in the cold water beneath. Probably, this property of liquid water, being denser than its solid form, ice, is unique among liquids. Also, life is not comfortable, save within the narrow limits of temperature of between about -10^0C and +55^0C. Note also, that although local changes are taking place continually, during 4,000 millions of years, the climate of the Earth has remained astonishingly uniform. This is due, in part, to the greater stability of the binary Earth-Moon system compared with that of the Earth by itself.

Yet much was needed to fit the Earth for human habitation, namely the chemical and physical preparation of its surface; the breaking of the rocks into soil, so that plants could take root and grow and provide food for the earliest animals. Even volcanoes assisted in the process by raising the surface and scattering, as dust, the deep-lying strata, rich in lime and phosphates, to form fertile plains. There seems to be a certain something to show that nature cares for the continuation of life.

How then are we to be distinguished from the rest? Superior intelligence perhaps, but it seems that we are merely creatures among innumerable others, from bacilli to elephants, inhabiting for a moment, a small planet, like a mote of dust, of a minor star, the Sun, itself like a diminutive firefly. We may be sure that for every human being in the World, there is not just one star apiece, there are ten thousand of them.

If nature gave us logic, she appears to be singularly lacking in what she bestows, exhibiting an inconsistency, which in a person would be accounted as madness. Her habit seems to turn upon herself. She sends hailstones to destroy her own blossoms and fruits. The sand of the desert, or the encroaching sea, turns fertile fields into barren wastes, reducing whole populations to distress, or starvation. In nature's speech there is equivocation, an irony clearly discerned. Note that this nature, which wars upon itself, is the same nature that has constructed the exquisite fabric of the living organism, and with a physician's art ministers to the diseases she inflicts, producing in the body anti-toxins to defeat the toxins. That nature should create a World full of difficulties and dangers, and thereupon to place within its fabric an infinite delicacy and complexity to meet these very dangers and difficulties, is a contradiction to baffle the understanding. What best nourishes, or what damages, the delicate machinery of nerve and brain? Poisons circulate in our blood from origins unknown. And indeed, our characters are no less vulnerable than our bodies. Our affections are thwarted, or forbidden, or we discover too late that they have been foolishly misplaced, and are destroyed. Our very sympathies can also lead us astray. Instinct and desire point one way, while mature reflection points to another. To live at all, without inflicting injuries upon others, is well-nigh, if not altogether, impossible. Insensitive nature remains insensitive to Earth's misery and looks down upon the interminable procession of the living to join the countless hosts of the dead. Unemotional, passionless nature has given birth to passionate, emotional man. The worst is that the World should be wholly senseless and without meaning, and this has happened. The power and energy of the Universe is doing nothing. It is lunatic, making and breaking, endlessly and aimlessly. The Universe is found wanting – its absence of mind and indifference to itself and to all its works and ways, is amazing. But man <u>does</u> think. Remove man and the vast machinery has no point. Thus time was, until recently, when our world <u>was not</u>, although our World is almost four billion years old! And nature has not changed. Life is a perilous adventure, and a perilous adventure for men (and for their empires) it will remain. Yet if man perishes, then still the ridiculous performance continues. It is extremely curious!

Yet it is the broken hearts that appal us. What elicits human horror and indignation, is not so much the suffering that the strong may with courage endure, as the suffering, at random, inflicted upon the weak, innocent and helpless. Nor would the heroic race of men, shrink from grief and wounds, were it only assigned a noble task. But nature prescribes none. To all our queries, nature never answers a word. The discovery of a goal is by far the most difficult task, but this she leaves to us. We must think, breathe and walk for ourselves, and although thinking is burdensome, nothing can extinguish our curiosity. But let's have laughter rather than holiness, beauty rather than birth (though, at times, these can go hand in hand) and common-sense, only if sheer nonsense is appreciated also. We choose our path, uncounselled, and at our own peril, and yet the unlikely track may still prove to be the best one.

Perhaps nature may have meant well by us, but could only give us second best. She could confer life, but not preserve it. But we may ask, "Was it really necessary that man's superiority should prove his bane and that his aspirations should end in death?" And there is another pervasive artifice of nature by which she induces us to invest in a future that we cannot hope to see. Why should hope have a place, heroism a place and renunciation a place, in this our automaton nature? Is cajolery among nature's talents? The Spartans at Thermopylae were flattered to their ruin by a ridiculous pride of race!

And yet, at the heart of existence, there lies an undeniable sweetness, which no philosophy has fathomed. As a result, Addison wanted us to consider the World in its most agreeable aspects. But the complaints against it are legion. "Vanity of vanities, all is vanity." All that exists is evil; so much for life; no value anywhere. So what sort of pessimist is this, who plays the flute? Even pessimists, philosophers and Christians marry and are given in marriage. They succumb, at times, to song and laughter. Cheerfulness keeps lurking in odd corners of the horrid gloom. Though not to be compared with the ineffable bliss we demand, but as an alternative to nothing, a case for existence can be stated. In fairness to life/nature, we must enter this natural sweetness into the ledger of our account of it. The ecstasy of lovers, the joy in activity, the glow, the radiance, the sunlight, the perfume – omit these and you have only drawn a caricature. There is music in the air. The adventurous and the courageous, somehow, are more inspiring than the defeatists.

"I think, therefore I am," said Descartes, as an undeniable proposition of his philosophic thought. His successors have found this to be either deniable, or insufficient. Alternatives such as, "I act," or "I desire," "therefore I am," similarly have been rejected. Pessimists have relieved us of our personality, freedom, souls and our very selves, but have left us our sorrows. Let us take as our proposition, "I suffer, therefore I am," and the converse, "I am, therefore I suffer." The privilege, if so it is, of existence/life is ours, and we hope that nothing can any longer intimidate us!

What kind of World is this that we inhabit? What are some of the possible, and alternative interpretations of things as they are?

We can begin with everyone's experience: we did neither make our natures nor their surroundings. Here we are in a state of being not of our own choosing and it is this astonishing situation for which we require some sort of explanation and/or interpretation (but we must beware of the danger for our logic when our affections, or interests, are involved!)

From the first to the last of our life's complicated situation, the stupefying fact is that we seem to be wholly in the dark about everything. Life and the World "beggar all description", let alone comprehension. Our business then, is not to solve problems beyond mortal powers, but to see to it that they are worthy of the task in hand. We could say that human affairs are hardly worth considering with any great seriousness, and yet we must be in earnest about them. Indeed, what else is there to be earnest about? Justice is justice, and tyranny is tyranny, whether a Sultan's or a God's. We are nature's children, her contradictions are ours and ours also her talents and graces.

These days, on every side, we meet with an exaltation of the intellect at the expense of the spirit. One may trust one's thoughts but not one's aspirations. Thought, truth and lies dwell only with those living creatures who have the use of speech. Unfortunately, there is a tremendous chasm between language and the reality of which it speaks. Words are clearly not the things themselves. Even more doubtful is whether shades of thought, let us say in French, can be expressed adequately in Chinese, and *vice-versa*. The most persuasive thought/force throughout history has been metaphor, or figurative expression. Man has lived by imagination. However, the human mind is not as philosophers would have us think, i.e. a debating hall, but rather a picture gallery. Certain opinions give satisfaction to some minds, which to others seem irrelevant and even meaningless. Historians are familiar with what are called, "climates of opinion". At another extreme, our minds may resemble a sea-shell, placed to our ear, in which the murmuring of the waves, is nothing more than that of our own blood. And so, reason may introduce us to a World as unreal as the shell heard sea.

Our times, in which we are privileged to live, are revolutionary, to brighten our intelligence. All the old conceptions, the belief in religion, in politics and in science, have been wholly transformed. But to accomplish anything at all, we need a genuine interest, a motive, or a centre for our thought. Knowledge has been the aim of our day and generation, and never has it been sought with greater determination, and never with greater success. In fact, we may even start to consider that man may be more interesting and important than his teachers desired him to be; possibly even a star of some magnitude within many a galaxy. Our admiration should be for man, and for his native power, his imagination, industry, ingenuity and understanding. Yet despite knowing more now than ever before, from which so much was hoped, we are concerned that we still know nothing of what we most wished to know. Presently, we exist in the Scientific Revolution. But science has failed to minister to our innermost needs for guidance and for understanding the complexities of the modern World.

Christianity has treated the whole animal kingdom with calm disdain. Indeed nineteenth men of science thought of nature as quite apart from, and outside of, ourselves; there for ages past, and there to be for ages to come. Early Christians had abandoned belief in the present World and had turned their thoughts to a better one to come. Everything that met the eye of medieval man seemed unintelligible unless it contained some deeper meaning than his senses revealed. This was his religion. But 400 years ago, during the Renaissance, men made discoveries that brightened their thoughts, and brought daylight, so that our ancestors were able to cross from the medieval into the modern World with fresh enthusiasm in their hearts. But these days, religion, e.g. Christianity, is fast descending into humanitarianism. This decrease in faith is due to the increase of our positive knowledge such that 'God' and the 'soul' are becoming extinct conceptions.

Our World now is a successful one of reason. When we think of mankind in general, we perceive how closely human destiny is associated with the pulsating energies of nature, of which we are, for the most part, utterly unconscious. Geologists tell Earth's story in terms of aeons. Continents float like rafts upon the Earth's surface. Archaeologists tell us about prehistoric man and of huge monsters, so that the affairs of 'homo-sapiens' belong only to yesterday. Light is a rapid messenger, yet it brings late news of cosmic events. A great flame in the heavens in 1901 took place, it is calculated, in 1551! What the telescope reveals today in the nebula of Andromeda is a story of happenings a million years ago. And how significant is the cycle of Sun-spots? From further afield, cosmic radiation pours down upon us from the most distant stars. Indeed, we are protected by Earth's atmosphere from a host of cosmic rays. Galactic distances and incredibly accurate atomic clocks enable us to date the laying of the foundations of our Universe. On the other hand, the World of micro-organisms, genetics and heredity are revolutionising medicine.

Electricity has been harnessed as a domestic slave. 'Live' television, in our own homes, lets us see and hear events the moment that they occur. Pilots have conquered the air, the stratosphere and have considered space travel, while divers show us the ongoing conquest of the oceans, all of which serves to amaze us.

All this foregoing has happened as the result of thinking and in this process it has also been turned upon ourselves. Our hidden portion, our murky basement, unknowingly determines our preferences. As intelligent beings, we are, in reality, it seems, swayed by primitive impulses and instincts. Man's character, as determined by his conscious thought, is gone. We have come to realise that transgressors of the social code are often sufferers, as well as malcontents. How profoundly psychological knowledge must modify our views of human life, and, in turn, the whole structure of our society.

Accordingly, we should ask whether man's intelligence is sufficient for his needs. Allegedly, thought and reason were the candle and a fragment-of-God. However, an active, inner principle (consciousness), wholly independent of the five senses, is essential for the process of obtaining knowledge. But revolutions, which began in the name of reason, have commonly ended in wholesale slaughter. Thought of a kind goes on all around us, yet who believes these days that Mahomet, or Luther, Robespierre, Hitler, or Stalin – all leaders of thought – were rational? Seemingly, human thought is worm-eaten with prejudice and fallacies. When people undertake to reason, it seems that all becomes lost. Even science sheds its last year's conclusions as a snake its skin; even perception, at best, can only be superficial.

Yet surely our understandings are equal, at least, to our near and immediate needs. Whatever else it may be, thought is an adjustment to its surroundings. Thought is a deposit of long human and racial experience of the World we inhabit, justified by its success and services to mankind. Thought is the slave of life. Yet despite its disadvantages, reasoning is all we have. "Cross-questioning" is the greatest and most efficacious of all purifications, so that, in its hospitable state, mind answers to mind. There is nothing so difficult as to lie beyond the reach of investigation, or so we believe. We can do very well with reason, but we are not to assume that what is now unknown is forever unknowable. "Reason 'till reason fail, 'till it discovers a power superior to its own." We must stand by that.

It is now time for us to look back. We desire to arrive at a true knowledge of the Universe, in which we exist. Of this Universe, man is a part, and indeed, from his own standpoint, its absolute centre. If we are to get to the root of things, it is not only the habits of nature that we must study, but also the habits of people. People themselves must be our teachers, people as they go about the World, and there reveal, naked and undisguised, the character of their species, in its motives, manners and actions. In history, we have a faithful mirror, which reflects the features of humanity. And by history, we mean the universal history of people. Is there anything new to be found in it? But nothing must be omitted from the vast, the perpetual, immense and innumerable goings-on of the visible World. 'A man of mild manners can form little idea of inveterate revenge, or cruelty.' There appears to be a maggot in every human brain. There is no need to visit a madhouse to find lunatics. So numerous are the illusions, frenzies and hallucinations afloat in the World that the Earth is the asylum of the Universe for the disordered minds. The insane delusions from which men suffer are beyond computation.

Thus, from a bird's eye view, history does not present our species in a very favourable light. The most troublesome thing in the World is the individual man. Many are his races and many the temperaments. As a consequence, history is the despair of philosophy because it consists of the doings of innumerable, unique and obstinate individuals. Their individual essence is wilfulness and their actions are unpredictable. Similarly, the data of science, derived from docile things and events, are susceptible to classification and assignable to laws – laws that govern many cases, and preferably all cases. Unfortunately, nature never repeats her patterns so that the human mind, nourishing a pattern for unification, is discomforted. There is no philosophy, or science, of unique, individual events.

More collectively, we may quote, "O Liberty, O Religion, what crimes have been committed in thy names!" The romance of war may be dead (it has become uglier and grimmer) and the pugnacity of the human species is especially the target of the moralists. Yet when mighty issues are at stake, will man remain unmoved? Will the cry of, "Truth, freedom and justice, though the heavens fall!" no longer be heard? Faith in absolute and eternal values makes this very unlikely.

In every part of the World, where the West's interests are at stake, we should be in favour of advancing them, even at the cost of war. If men and nations do not find life worth living, or of what it offers worth possessing, it is very certain that nature will replace them by others who do. The spirit of giving in, is the most fatal disease to which nations are subject, and is apt to attack them like a cancer, when they have arrived at the meridian. If the heart be set on nothing that the Earth contains, or offers, then nothing in the manner of the Earth will be done there. Let us think no more about look-warm neutrals, but look once and pass on.

When the West's day comes to an end, the principles that contributed to its coming, will not be strengthened. On the contrary, they will be eclipsed and dissolved with the triumph of opposing principles. The decline and fall of the West, which will rejoice its enemies, will not be the West's decline and fall, but of all for which it stood, and not until then shall we know the extent of our miseries. The West, at least, is not of the opinion that humanity, justice, freedom or religion will be the gainers in that fall.

War has been the moralist's great industry. Abolish it and you will have abolished mankind's worst feature. Yet it is not only war that is a matter of life and death; economic sanctions make war by starvation. Trade and commerce are matters of life and death to millions. If oil becomes the necessary and universal fuel, then the oil producing countries flourish at the expense of those who have none. The Liverpool merchants sold three hundred thousand slaves within twelve years for fifteen million pounds. Through economic competition, waged with an easy conscience, we have a longer and less noble form of war and no less ruthless. Capture a nation's markets and you strike at its life. Everything is what it is, and not another thing. However, when we have added the catastrophes of famine, flood, earthquake and fire, then nature has been just as disastrous to our species, as from our species itself.

Also, the fecundity of nature is a huge enemy. As wide as the World is, it is far from spacious, so narrow are the limits of habitable land. Nor are its resources inexhaustible. There is not room upon the Earth for a tithe of the creatures that desire to possess it. All living things multiply as long as they can find sustenance. We shall need to establish birth control universally among all of them, so that our goal of survival may then be secured. Civilisations belong in moderate, not torrid, zones. Civilisations arise at a price, and large populations place a heavy toll on the countries they inhabit. Whatever nature intended, manifestly it was not that we should exist as mere pensioners upon her bounty. Vast migrations of peoples probably will take place in the future, as they have in the past, and the hunger, etc., for them, will not diminish.

Overall, if we are honest, life is not a great price to pay. To account for our own passionate attachment to living is not easy. The Earth has spawned millions upon millions of sapiens. Of their passage across the stage, the majority have left no trace. 'They were, and are not', is their only epitaph.

Human sentiment has always honoured men cast in the heroic mould, the strong men of their lands, who brought death to thousands as they waded through blood to their own desired goals. Great deeds are not done by desiring nothing. Words like Destiny and Fate, as rulers of mortal things for reflective folk like the Greeks, or the Northmen, are seldom heard today, but their power has not abated.

But if we should wish to know our World, then perhaps we should ask about its luxuries and frivolities. Where the heart is, that is where the money goes. The extravagances of Oriental monarchs and of Roman emperors, are proverbial. Even so, a comparison of the expenditure involved, with that of the present day, might not be to our advantage. Yet man's inventive and architectural faculties are equally in evidence. He has also founded empires, laws and constitutions, the arts of government and peace. Seemingly, he is composed of "fleeting opposites".

Let us give to man and his science their due. Science does provide us with a strong means of distinguishing between the precise and the qualitative, and so imparts some consistency and organisation. The very peculiar qualities of oxygen, hydrogen and carbon made a habitable World possible. If these three major elements in combination built up the many million varieties of living organisms, how then did oxygen, hydrogen and carbon obtain their singular power of co-operating, constructing and organising their combination together to produce a unity? Whence did all this come from, and where does it reside?

Modern science teaches that nature's energy doesn't operate in a continuous, unbroken current, but is discontinuous, i.e. periodic and rhythmical, or wavelike and particulate. Consciousness, in some form, is found where life is found: dreaming as in plants, half-awake as in animals, or wide-awake as in ourselves. It too, is both intermittent and recumbent. Thus, it is by way of a staircase, and not a slope, that man has attained his eminence.

Who can be blind to the advances of science concerning life-expectation? But no-one can yet tell us why we grow old, stiffen and die, save that such is the rhythm of existence.

The first and inescapable question is the simple one of acceptance (or rejection) of life, not as one would like it, but as it is under our prevailing conditions. And what of life itself? It appears to be the result of the backwash of the tide of energy that produced the solar system. But the Sun and star galaxies were not in need of the society of living things. They were not restless, unhappy and lonely, wanting someone to talk to. The Universe could have done very well without them and their society, as they bring no obvious profit to the sum of things. Why then, are they here?

On the other hand, life reproduces itself, a very clever trick, so that life, in our experience, arises only from previous life. Thus, inheritance is the most obvious fact taught by observation. From our ancestors, we inherit the country to which we belong, its laws and customs, its institutions and social regime. Also, we inherit from them our bodies, our sex and the fashion of our features, such as the colour of our eyes, our skin and our hair, while not forgetting our very dimples. In addition, we inherit the genes upon whose composition, combination and distribution everything depends. Does anyone suggest that we made any of these things, or have any responsibility for them? But now, "All are but parts of one stupendous whole, whose body nature is." As the organism needs an environment, so the environment, if there needs to be life, needs an organism. They belong to each other and work together. They are indeed, manifestly one, with an understanding between them. The inhabitants of the Earth form one family. Life is one.

So what can we say about these all-powerful genes? They are the units of the characteristics upon which heredity depends. They cannot be seen but within a germ-cell there is a nucleus, which consists of chromosomes, visible through a microscope, and within them lie the conjectured genes that carry all the heritable qualities. Thus, each individual is no more than a bundle of inherited characteristics. Since extracts from the thyroid and pituitary glands have the power to dislocate, or to restore, personality; our bodily life seems to consist very much of a matter of chemistry.

Individual cells consist of a world in themselves; of filaments, globules and residues, all with their own particular functions and all in perpetual agitation, which, in turn, are superimposed upon the far deeper, unseen vibrations of molecules, which comprise the ultra-microscopic foundations of the whole physico-chemical system. Scientists like to think that genes themselves are physico-chemical structures and that life arose in a chemical ferment.

In talking about cells, biologists talk in numbers that remind us of the astronomers and the stars. A drop of water confounds us. It contains millions upon millions of molecules. In fact, all of matter, in its atoms, consists only of electrons, protons and neutrons – a tremendous unification/simplification. Each liver cell in our bodies contains three hundred billion atoms. At a higher level, then, all of life consists of cells – another tremendous unification/simplification. We seem to be, one and all, constellations, within which we have the cells of the brain, of the liver, and of the stomach; each variously engaged upon its own separate tasks and yet all working in harmony to keep our bodies healthy and alive.

We might have supposed that within the living cell, there were parts corresponding to the different portions, or organs, of the body-to-be. As Leibniz taught, the original cell, or egg, was already the animal to come, on a microscopic scale. But nothing so simple; that is not nature's way. The germ-cell is a unity and does not become specialised for the production of the heart, or lungs, or any other part of the body, until it has attained a certain maturity. If, at an early stage, the cell becomes divided, or is subject to pressure, or even if a portion is removed, the germ-cell retains all its powers. Astonishingly, it can provide any, or all, necessary organs, out of any part of itself. The cells, too, in living things, can act for each other, and work together, for a common purpose. The co-operation of parts is everywhere present in natural organisms. What governs the procedure? Who, or what, presides over the organisation? Where dwells the wisdom in the germ-cell capable of detecting deficiencies in itself, when they arise; where the intelligence, simulated or otherwise, which can transfer to the remaining parts, duties previously performed by others? We would think that a germ-cell would hardly be aware that it had lost a portion of itself, and would carry on blindly, quite unconscious of any injury, or defect, it had sustained. But this pin-point of matter contains within itself the power to become a human being, with all its organs complete – brain, heart and lungs.

Also, the germ-cell contains within itself the power to develop the eye, the ear, the will, the emotions and the thoughts that make a person. Additionally, it contains the power of reproducing its kind, of recalling the features, the smile, the complexion, the tricks of speech, the grace of carriage that characterise the parent stock.

Let us consider the eye alone. How insignificant a trifle it is. Yet it is a triumph of nature, possessing powers that the lordly constellations desperately lack. Its germ-cell contains the ability to produce a retinal surface sensitive to light between wavelengths of 450 – 750 milli-microns, i.e. between the sensations of violet and red. How does it come about that the human eye responds to a certain series of wavelengths among a huge series of others? You would be inclined to say that this was a miracle, but miracles do not happen. Can you satisfy yourself that this accomplishment arose out of a haphazard compilation of atoms in a white-hot gas at temperatures of a million degrees, i.e. out of an incandescent maelstrom of darting electric flashes? Can you be satisfied that any evolutionary theory can, juggling with genes, account for life and mind?

How can we ignore the question, "To what end, or for what purpose, was the eye, or any other organ, developed?" If you propose to account for the eye, for example the need for it, its value must be considered. To suppose it an accidental variation, is sheer absurdity. This is because it appeared in more than one line of evolution. The cuttlefish and the unrelated vertebrates, both developed eyes on their own account in different ways, and from different parts of the organism. In addition, some fish provide a bifocal arrangement for sight not only in water but also in air. Moreover, a bird's eye view is adapted for both near and far vision and finally, a butterfly's eye contains 5,000 lenses and 50,000 nerves. These various eyes were means to certain definite ends, so that, in each case, the creature might have a visual advantage, especially suited to its own way of life. How can the 'immanent end', this internal teleology, be explained?

Organisms behave as if they had an end in view. They aim at self-preservation; their actions have a purpose, which they appear to be unconscious of, and yet strain after, to attain it (see 'The Selfish Gene' by R. Dawkins). An animal is interested in its environment and continually attends to, and adapts itself, to the changing scene. How can we ascribe interest to a blind, mechanical process? The activity of an organism is not motiveless. Biologists continually ask, "What end does this organ, eye or ear, the heart, or muscle, serve in the animal economy?" Organs that no longer serve a purpose degenerate and disappear. The body is the outcome of its wants, adapted to strive after and to serve them. A growing thing is known by what it grows into.

When we approach the lower boundaries of life, organisms become progressively smaller and more numerous. Bacteria are as the sands of the seashore in multitude – some harmful and some beneficial. But smaller still are the viruses, the filter-passers, which produce more deadly diseases, but may not be described as living creatures.

Above the bacteria, we have the single-celled animals. Each living thing begins as a single cell, which, following nutrition, grows and divides, and again divides, etc. until, in the various animals, from the amoeba, a single-celled creature, to man, the number of cells rises to millions and billions. If nothing hindered the sub-divisions of the amoeba, its descendants would, in a week, equal the Earth in size. Yet if the amoeba was just the size of a dog, no-one would deny to its actions, the name of intelligence.

Note that the impulse to mating, and the emphasis on sex, comprise two of nature's aims. How do we account for them? The body in higher animals, develops from the union of two cells, the sperm and the ovum, contributed respectively by the father and mother, so that out of the 46 chromosomes for man, each parent contributes 23, but with a certain difference in one pair of male chromosomes, called x and y; x produces a girl baby and y, a boy one. No two germ-cells are alike, and the combination of a single sperm and ovum may give rise to an immense variety of patterns. Thus, we are partners in a gigantic lottery. From a single marriage, any one of innumerable, differently equipped, variously endowed individuals, may come into existence. Yet if some men are born with a silver spoon in their mouths, others enter the world with a millstone around their necks.

Manifestly, we are self-conscious beings. However, we must believe that our parents might have had many other and quite different children, wholly unlike us, each child possessed of, and each endowed with, peculiarities of its own, as well as with its same sense of personality. And similarly, their parents before them, might have had quite other children, as might their forebears, from the birth of heredity. In each family, a few, a very few, out of legions of possible human beings, have come into existence. Let us assume that they are among the favoured few. Why were they, like ourselves, so singled out? And at what moment, did this self of ours, this precious 'I', this individual person, attach itself to the chromosomes, from which we have sprung? There seems no reason why any particular 'I' should ever have entered into this World, or life.

The physiology of our physical structures tells us of hormones, like adrenalin and insulin, which generate fear and alleviate diabetes, respectively. It tells us of vitamins, which in the right dosage are necessary constituents of a healthy diet. Also, it tells us of the ductless glands, of the pituitary in particular, because it lies close to the brain, because it regulates growth and reproduction and because, if stimulated, produces a giant, and, if starved, a dwarf. Additionally, certain characteristics occur among first-born children. Moreover, left-handedness occurs more often in criminals, and is associated with dumbness. Furthermore, feeble-minded types occur more at the end of a family (King Edward II was a sixteenth child); colour-blinded men are more common than colour-blinded women, and that from some diseases, like haemophilia, women are exempt. So far then, from being intellectually, or morally, above our environment, we appear to be its slaves. We become angry, or agreeable, reasonable or unreasonable, as our environment dictates.

We arrive then at the integrity of the organism. In living, there is an agency at work. Leibniz defined an organism as anything that had a 'soul', or principle of unity, which he thought was in the nature of a force, rather than of a substance, or quality. This inner being of an organism exhibits all the marks by which we recognise 'consciousness' in ourselves.

Only one thing is left to us: our duty, which society insists upon, takes a firm grip of and with which, stands no nonsense. Our duty then, is the pivot of our society. Whether we are a bundle of inherited qualities, or not, whether we have free-will, or not, we are nonetheless responsible. Fortunately, most of us never doubt, or disclaim, responsibility. It is only if we can suppose that amid all that we patently do inherit, there is in each of us something personal and ungiven implanted in us, over which we have indisputable control (which we <u>can</u> suppose, see later), otherwise human existence becomes just a vast inconsequence.

We have to perceive the necessity of mind that upon its operations, recognitions and appreciations all hinges; that in thought, you have the end, the aim and the justification of nature. In effect, there is no Universe without an intelligence to be aware of it. Our opinion has become that life, consciousness and mind have not strayed accidentally into the Universe. There never was a cosmos without life. It is among its attributes, a constituent of its innermost being.

Meanwhile, we discover that we are still confined to the sensible World, to the clear, bright World, of which our touch, sight and hearing tell us. Yet curtain after curtain might lift and still leave us far from reality. The truth is that we are so cabined, cribbed and confined, as never to see beyond our noses. Nor is that all. If we could enlarge our minds to see that even a national drama is no more than 'a three hours traffic of the stage' in unending time, then the long vista of things, the magnitude of the affair in which we are involved, might come home to us. The sum of things is too great for our imaginations, and our present lives seem like terms of imprisonment. In a measure, perhaps this is so.

We expect that the work of God should be without a flaw. Yet the World appears to be at war with itself and to be ruled by rival powers, such as God and Satan, who both seem to be in evidence. Possibly, it is this clash of opposites that has brought the World about in the first place, so that we are fortunate, perhaps, to have a World at all. The laws of polarity [Heraclitus] constituted the inner thought, or the supreme principle of the World, rather like the Chinese Yin (negative) and Yang (positive). Possibly, this sort of philosophy could accurately reflect our "Human Situation".

CHAPTER 2

OUR SIMPLE 1940 A.D. SITUATION

Abstracted and Rearranged from
'The Human Situation' by
W. MacNeile Dixon.

Part 2 – mainly immaterial.

<u>General.</u> The first step in philosophy is to open our eyes. In part 1 we tried to recall the magnitude of the World/Universe, our dwelling, the vast scale of its spatial and temporal dimensions; the violence and inconsistency of nature; the singular character of human life, its vicissitudes, varieties, affiliations, contrarieties, the contending currents and the sound, light and darkness of the sea of circumstances, for which we give the name of history.

Now for a more perplexing region. To the question, "What does human experience tell us?" is added another, "How came this strange experience to be ours?" and again, "What is its purpose, or meaning, if it have any?" and "What is to be made of it?" Now we have got more than enough on our hands! We are supposed to attempt an account of everything, of all existence, but particularly of "consciousness", one of the faculty of knowing, feeling and being interested in anything. We are to try to account for will and desire, love and hate, for philosophy, art, music, science and religion, for stars and their systems, for good and evil, for Newton's *'Principia'* and for Shakespeare's plays.

The mind is certainly a part of reality, but the part is not the equal of the whole. That man can set about an enquiry into his own origins, and should succeed, is itself fantastic, and possibly insane. We may journey and never arrive. The obstacle to our comprehension of the nature and structure of our World, is nowhere else than in us. Our instrument at hand is philosophy, neither greatly triumphant, nor much in demand.

Early among our experiences, we will have met with disappointment. Despite a certain plasticity, there is a rigidity to the World's structure, not of our making. To have a regard for what is possible here, is therefore the beginning of wisdom. By all means let us worship perfection, but do not ask for, or expect, it. We conclude that the condition of our lives simply does not permit of the untold felicity of which we crave, and can never permit of it. Utopian dreamers all, have misread the map, and so will remain forever lost in the mountains of 'No-man's land'.

Let us assume as little as possible, and begin with things as we find them. They are neither greatly to our liking, nor is the Earth, as a residence, particularly recommended. Its inhabitants are hardly described in enthusiastic terms either. "What can you tell me about Winchester?" asked the traveller of the coach's driver. "Debauched, sir," came the reply, "like all Cathedral cities."

If we are embodied souls, then it remains to be understood why they are embodied. Presumably nature produced bodies that serve some end; something of importance, or some necessity, is represented. How mystics proposed to get along without a body, we cannot tell. The human body has been abused beyond measure. How much better, or worse, would we have been without, say, an unruly member, like the tongue? St. Francis spoke kindly of 'Brother Body – the Ass'. But its vices are legion. It harbours fleshly lusts, which war against the soul. Why then, was it thrust upon us? If it was either a worthless, or a doubtful friend, or an enemy, then by what kind of fate are we so afflicted? Suspiciously, bodily wishes, affections and hopes have so much more apparent naturalness than the so-called spiritual. Any system of thought that leaves out our flesh and blood, leads fatally to a swamp of contradictions, because they quarrel with the fundamental nature of things. They must be taken as they are, explained so, or not at all.

We have seen reason to think that the World is what it is, out of necessity, if a World there was to be. It has a structure, to which, as to the structure of our bodies, we must submit willy-nilly. It imposes upon us the sharpest limitations and restrictions. We cannot breathe under water, or fly unaided in the sky. We are implanted with several, ineradicable, irresistible appetites and desires. Simply, we cannot have it all our own way, either with the World, or with ourselves.

Thinking, upon its arrival, discovered the perplexities of the World, propounded the problems and then itself had to explain to us, our human situation.

The word 'spirit' is, in our language, set above matter. But on what grounds are terrestrial things so maligned? Is the 'interior', meditative man a higher type of being than the busy, 'exterior' man? Things are, by no means, that simple. Similarly, we hear sometimes of 'holiness'. Does this consist of a capacity for awe, reverence, and some kind of cosmic emotion? How then does it qualify for eternal happiness?

The World has produced mind in man. No-one really knows how – but, strange to relate, in this mind has arisen a critic, who comments insolently on his creator, if a creator there be – a somewhat singular situation – like a dog at its master, or as a thankless child rebukes its parent. The mind turns upon the World, of which it is a part, and declares that the whole design is a bungled business. Is an evil god speaking through the human mind, since the World's creator can't be supposed to reprobate his own creation?

Our position is that the World's imperfections are inherent in its necessary and unavoidable structure. On the other hand, philosophers declare that the imperfections have no real existence; they are merely human, short-sighted illusions. But theologians admit their reality and ascribe them to sinful man. Yet most observers agree that something needs to be done urgently. Generally, the World falls short of humanity's requirements. To disapprove of the World as a spectacle would seem hypercritical. But to live in the World, and to be subject to all its accidents, is different from viewing it through an opera glass.

To the human intellect, the World is a veritable delirium, where there is little room for logic, and as for reason, nothing at all. When human thought meets with movement, change and many separated things, it becomes utterly defeated. Unless they can be pigeon-holed, ticketed, or classified, they cannot be firmly laid hold of, and so become abhorrent. Rest and changelessness seem to us, the proper and natural situation of things, as they should be. Our minds have two bugbears, and two heart's idols: the bugbears are change and manyness; its heart's idols are permanence and unity. And so, theologians and moralists recoil from changing things, and demand the stationary and immutable. To understand the World, its dizzying movement must be stopped. Then we can begin to understand it. Unity of the whole, must, in some way, be attainable. But the World does not provide such a vision, since it presents disunion, separateness, multiplicity and incessant change, i.e. a stupefying chaos.

Throughout the World, everything appears to be at odds, in collision with some other thing; one energy opposes another, growth strives against decay; life battles with death and men antagonise other men. Nowhere in this den of antipathies, is found a semblance of order, permanence, harmony and unity of hearts and ideals, so deeply, we think, to be desired. Apart from keeping alive, with the 'purse' to do it, what a trial, even in good times, we are to each other. Where does a perfect World, untroubled by contraries exist; where discord, change, or disunity, are unknown? Why did nature, with no satisfaction in her everlasting toil, ever undertake to produce it? Heaven knows! No-one seems pleased! However, there is a country of blessed union with the serene and immutable One. All you have to do to enter it, is to die!

Yet, for the present, here we are, with our dreams and plans to improve our temporary surroundings. Those, indeed, who find life and the World pleasingly attractive as they are, have no need of dreams. At rare moments, existence has seemed better than non-existence, as in the palmy days of Greece, or England. What vigour, briskness and vivacity men displayed, with what crisp convictions they conversed and acted upon. But the World has known other men and moods. "What devilry is here?" they cry, "What is the worth of all these brutal triumphs?" These sages of the heaven-born, are far wiser, more spiritual and profound than the rest of us.

Stoic thought says that we have no power at all over outward things, because they are too strong and because there is no logic in their proceedings. Nature is irrational, immoral and lacks respect for its victims. But man's rational mind is an independent kingdom, over which material things, or nature, for all their brutal strength, have no sovereignty. Man can look down upon atrocities, miseries and wickedness with contempt, and so rule them. If his soul's condition is sound, and if he cares not whether he is well or ill; in prison or on the rack; whether or not his friends and children die; his country perishes and if he, himself, lives or dies; if he can view all such things as unconcernedly as he watches a leaf fall, then he may, indeed, claim divinity. Of all the World rejection creeds, Stoicism has the proudest and grandest air.

But we can ask, "Are these fugitives from life on the path of wisdom?" Does the power that produced them, require them, during their brief life on Earth, to sacrifice all natural joys and affections upon the altar of negation? At times, few of us can withhold our astonished admiration for the unflinching courage, which men have shown, following their beliefs. On the other hand, religion and morals have had their fanatics, and their desperadoes, who will stop at nothing. Not only have these men inflicted injuries upon others, but have also let loose terrible fury upon themselves. What wild dreams have they harboured? What lunacies have they not derived? In the process, they have made of life, the hell that they have tried to escape.

The praises of solitude have often been sung. There, even while an Earth-dweller, you are told you enter Nirvana, and its heavenly silence, as in the grave, where you will never more be disturbed.

Whereas the extremist finds his chief delight in society, in the cheerful stir and animation, in family relationships, in carnival meetings, in banter and debate; the introvert seeks his pleasure in retirement, in the loneliness where all discords die away and all babblings cease. Hence, we find the opposites everywhere, the contending currents both in the World without, as well as within the World of thought.

Contraries are implicit in the World's structure [Heraclitus] and without them there would be no World. Excesses, defects and contrary qualities conspire to the beauty and harmony of the World. Men see things from their own angles – time and place – in conformity with their own experience and individualities – the lonely vision of each. It is the same World, the same landscape, which amazes, horrifies, or delights its inhabitants, so dissimilar are hearts and minds.

The Will-to-Live. Yet whatever the drawbacks of our undesirable neighbourhood, or where we might least expect to find it, we always meet up with the will-to-live. Behind all the storms and confusion, above the hurrying to and fro; the protestations and proclamations, sits, enthroned in silence, the inscrutable and mysterious will-to-live. This will-to-live is ubiquitous, universal and insistent. All existence manifests it, life in every creature exemplifies it and well we know it in ourselves. The hounds of this desire to be alive, and to remain so, are in full cry. It is more fundamental than thought, or mind, and gave birth to the whole creation. It is everywhere, and at every moment in frank and open evidence. Yet reason offers little explanation for this corner-stone of our being. This mysterious prompting to continue living, to remain in the World, is, by common consent, well-nigh invulnerable, and of all our instincts, the most difficult to dislodge, or to subdue.

Achilles said that he preferred to be an earthly serf, or drudge, than to live in the underworld of the dead. Patently, the will-to-live cannot be derived from a source in our surroundings. On the contrary, it meets with all kinds of discouragement. Yet somehow, the most convinced pessimists are in no haste to die. The will-to-live holds its own even against the well-to-do professors of misery. The will-to-live has no doubts about life's value. With doubts about life's value, our fellow creatures, the lower animals, are placidly unconcerned. No animal questions it. And so, there is a mystery - the quarrel of life with the conditions of life, and the revolt of mankind.

The will-to-live is invariably lodged, or embodied, in separate, individual organisms. Thus arises the struggle for existence, and, in turn, the strife. The plants make use of the material elements, they are consumed by animals, and they by others stronger than they, including man, the master of them all. Finally, we reach the level of conscious intelligence in man, as homo-sapiens. The intellect arrives, and, strange to tell, contentment fades. With the dawn of intelligence, and not until then, arise the dark suspicions of the worth of life.

The will-to-live may be accused, placed on trial, found guilty of all human misery and sentenced to death. Since the worthlessness of life is a conclusion, not only of a few discontented malcontents, but also from the experience of multitudes, we cannot pass it by negligently. Yet it may be said that the charge of utter senselessness against the sum of things, demands a strong advocate. To convict nature of inferiority to ourselves, we creatures of a day, will need some pleading. However good the case, invectives against living carry little conviction. To be, in order not to be, is scarcely an alluring proposal. Thus, the World will remain worldly and not wear a hair-shirt all life long, if only for the possible reason that the fugitives from life, such is nature's cunning, leave few descendants, so that their kind perishes.

To tell human beings that they are already, at birth, dead men, as if they had not enough to put up with; that they were ushered into being, in order to turn and rend themselves; is a doctrine that the majority are unlikely to accept. It will seem to them, what it is, a doctrine of the tongue, and not of the heart, a plaything of the fool, just to pass the time. Let us ask ourselves, what is the type of people, who have made history? We shall answer that they have not been World denunciators; the cause for which they fight is a lost one. And if we hold empires, states, civilisations, arts and sciences worth the building, then this requires more than the saving of the individual soul by communion with eternal things. For nations, meekness is not a virtue, but a contemptible, dangerous vice. While we live, let us live. Considering the stupendous panorama of the World, it is a sulky and sullen humour that cries out upon it all, "Get thee behind me, Satan!"

The will-to-live, in ourselves, is the undying, the incorruptible witness to nature's will. Whence, or why, comes the never countermanded order to every living thing, to fulfil its being and so remain in existence? There is something, said Shelley, in man at enmity with nothingness and dissolution.

In addition, the will-to-live points beyond the present. We are not in nature's confidence but we are mysteriously upheld by some secret influence. In us, some project is at work, some end foreshadowed. It is the will-to-live that has given birth to human love, to human art, to the soul's ideals and to its hope of immortality. Why turn away from this simple and evident truth? Shrouded though it is in mystery, the will-to-live speaks out of the depths, and is less concerned with what is, than with what is to be. Under its guidance, our race has become wiser than its instructors, has declined to sit with them in ashes, and has continued to say to life, "Good morning, you are welcome."

In two instants: the will-to-live, emanating from the darkness, whence we came; and hope, a shining light in advance of us; nature speaks to us from her depths. If history has any meaning, then we are upon a voyage hardly yet begun. But what comes next? Do we live for eternity, or for our own time? However, there is no living for eternity except in time, and nor can this be supported without the resolution: 'to strive, to seek, to find and not to yield.' And to those in alarm, either for themselves, or for the ship of humanity, we could do well to remember St. Paul's words to the trembling gaoler, "Do thyself no harm, for we are all here."

On the other hand, how deep and natural is the instinct that all our desires should be fulfilled at once. Even the cradled child weeps at the oppositions to its every wish. "How do we justify," men asked, "our own seizure of the best, or how can the conflicting purposes, their own with all the others, be harmonised, strife evaded, hatreds avoided, wars ended and unbroken happiness attained?" These difficulties have yet to be resolved. In our desperation, should we, in our turn, go the way of the East, praying for deliverance from the wheel of existence, and turn our backs upon the ambitions and pursuits of contending nations?

Until recently, Confucianism maintained three hundred million Chinese based on its philosophy, religion and ethical system. What was this powerful teaching? It was secularism – the creed of good manners and gentlemanly behaviour. It said nothing about God, the supernatural, or about a future existence. Before the oriental despot, men prostrated themselves in the dust. The Oriental stands for peace at the price of submission; the Ancient Greek for freedom at the price of combat. The difference is the choice between the slave and the free man. Please note that there were no conscientious objectors among the Spartans, no sentimentalists among the Red Indians, no saints among the Vikings, no pacifists among the Japanese, no hermits in Greenland, and no World despisers in Mexico, or in the Argentine.

Life has summoned many men to heroic endeavour, has also driven many to despair and self-destruction and has made others half-mad for the love of God Is it possible that Saint Theresa, or John of the Cross, lived in the same World as us?

Also contrast the middle ages with the centuries that followed them. How different their respective visions of the World, how opposed their systems of belief. Yet each was held as inevitable and unassailable in its time.

Now consider the naturalists. They ask, "Why should we try to escape, or transcend, life as we find it? It is there to be savoured and enjoyed. Be content. Why regard this life as insufficient, or spend yourself in labour for thankless successors, or strive after a heaven, of which we lack information?" Doctor Schweitzer argued that, as the will-to-live advances to a higher insight, it turns away from the hideous and intolerable conflict, thereby gaining an inner independence. Resign the glittering goods of the outer and passing World and resignation brings peace. But this is the well-worn path of the ascetics. Yet how difficult it is to distinguish its accents from those of terror and despair. Distrust of life, aversion from life and fear of life– what a sparkling trio of friends these are to accompany one upon any expedition! Thus, each age thinks itself in possession of the true and only view possible for sensible men.

Perhaps we may agree that life, for most people, has its moments. There are persons and actions that approach perfection, graces and beauties worth seeing, and days on which it is a happiness to be alive. But it is neither on these bright points that the argument hinges, nor upon the truth that the contraries constitute the web and woof of things, but rather upon the decision of whether or not the command of the will-to-live comes from a god, or from a devil. To our preposterous race, obstacles are the breath of life. We tend to reject the easy and the obvious and delight in exertions and pains. Give humans a task and a cause, and the harder, the better. They rise to the occasion, but ask nothing of them and they become captious, querulous and resisting.

If we could think that we have neither come from nothing, nor will return to nothing, that time has wide margins so that we can focus on a far distant goal, and so postpone our condemnation of both nature and man, then man, being hardly yet awake, might keep his soul alive, and thus not end in blank despair.

Three things, at least, have not yet been proved, that: 1) nature has exhausted herself in producing what she has; 2) all modes of being, i.e. of existence, lie open to the inspection of our physical senses and 3) the human mind has reached the zenith of its powers.

None of these is believable. The justification of life consists, not in increasing the felicity that we fondly fancy, but in providing, here and now, the infinity of its possibilities for the endless variety of its individual members, the happiness it offers despite its pains, and in the inextinguishable hope, as invincible as its sadness, which illuminates creation throughout its vast circumference.

<u>The Will-to-Live and Religion, Theology, Ethics and Morals.</u> The will-to-live in human beings is not on good terms with religion, theology ethics and morals [R, T, E & M]. These incline to see the will-to-live as the enemy both of God and of society. The principle of the will-to-live is to do the best for oneself, always and everywhere, which necessarily brings one into conflict with everyone else. It is the incarnation of selfishness (i.e. the selfish gene). R, T, E & M deplore this egoism and would have us abandon our pursuit of private goods and separate desires. They stand for unanimity, peace and law and order against the capricious, self-willed person. Unless he is curbed, or converted, how can society be saved from endless alarms, dangers and disturbances? How else can we sleep in security and comfort? Also, in the powerful will-to-live, we have nature speaking simply. The conflict is nothing short of desperate. R, T, E & M readily speak of men's delinquencies, but of the delinquencies of nature, of

which our will-to-live is a manifest product, they rarely complain, because this goes perilously close to judging God adversely, which, basically, is impossible. Even to combat nature is difficult (since we are surrounded by devouring and pitiless forces) and how well we know how merciless nature can be and how terrible her disasters. Nature produced her victims (her own children!) and can massacre them. This is the flaming paradox.

Yet R, T, E & M have neither produced any light on our situation, nor have they revealed the cause of our sufferings. For the pains of life they offer remedies, but when we ask why we have to endure them, they are silent, providing no explanation. Instead of criticising nature, we are told that we are chiefly responsible for our own sufferings. Yet when we think about this, we are not so sure that malice, hatred and lack of charity are the sole causes of our tribulations. Who now, does not see that if the purpose of God be represented by nature, then there is an impassable crevasse caused by the dislocation and cleavage between nature, the life-giver, and our R, T, E & M? Of nothing in the wide World are we the creators. The will-to-live is given to us, like everything else, and is not of our making. Yet observe how sure it is, and without hesitations.

To love life is to obey the will-to-live, and in that way we are fulfilling divine orders. This is to be found in all creatures as they set forth on their great expedition. But, as we have said, there are other beings in the World beside ourselves, to whom the same orders have been issued. The opportunity is the greater to exercise our brains. For a miracle has happened. We have exchanged nothingness for the possibility of everything. Yet this everything is only a bare possibility, and to implement it demands all the powers of body, mind and spirit at their highest tension. Existence has this advantage over non-existence: it denies nothing and leaves room for unimaginable experiences. But there will be misadventures among them. Existence is an oxymel, a bitter sweet. Yet exhilaration accompanies all creatures, a zest for living wells up in them, which it is too monstrous to deny. We have energies; nature has seen to that. But upon what are they to be expended? That, nature appears to have left to us.

In countering the will-to-live, R, T, E & M find themselves not only in opposition to nature, but also among the adversaries of life, the World deserters and despisers. They invite us to deny our natures and go out of existence. Is R, T, E & M's true message, however cloaked with eloquent phrases, that the less we have to do with life in the World, the wiser and nobler we shall be? Looking back through history, we can see how slight has been the success of R, T, E & M, but they have been helped by a secret ally in the human soul, namely the will-to-love.

The strong will-to-live is not easily set aside, but the will-to-love is an influence made up from our ideals of perfection. It is to our need for truth, goodness and beauty that R, T, E & M make their appeal. The source of our will-to-love, just like the source of our will-to-live, is hidden from us, yet both speak with authority and persuasiveness.

Throughout history mankind has been haunted by the question of at whose door we shall lay our troubles. That we ourselves are responsible for our troubles is preposterous. Our critical attitude towards the powers above, is sufficient evidence of the profound discordance found throughout the ages and felt among all peoples, of the disharmony between their desires/dreams and resistances everywhere. If we have reached the conclusion that the World is an iron-bound mechanism, then we might as well close our churches and put away our books of devotion. To worship a machine is no better than obeisance before a graven image. Yet men still cling to the idea that the powers above regard us with a friendly eye. However, they have not always been of that opinion. Not until the advent of Christianity was there a doctrine of a loving God, a benefactor of all mankind. Had life contented us, we should have been in heaven already. Not needing to seek happiness and to persuade men that their creator was a God of love, has proved an embarrassing and not too successful an undertaking. However, don't tell us that the will-to-believe was absent. The desire for a protecting providence is writ large in human history. But our minds cannot take kindly to magnificence unrelated to wisdom, and to grandeur divorced from soul. Humanity will have it that the omnipotence and benevolence should be somewhat in alliance.

Cardinal Newman's *'Apologia'* concluded that either there is no creator, or that the living society of men is in a true sense discarded from his presence. Newman did not stay to ask himself whether any other World was possible other than that of the contraries. He assumed its possibility. He also assumed that a perfect World had, at one time, actually existed. A perfect World seemed to him the only natural World, whereas our part in it, the actual, existing World, was unnatural and incomprehensible. Newman was convinced of God's existence and that he was good in a human sense and kind towards his creation. In his *'Apologia'*, we see that a pious soul is speaking. His words are not those of our bright optimists, who, with a few coats of humanitarian paint, will turn the Earth for you into heaven. Either there was no Creator, or the human race was implicated in some terrible aboriginal calamity, i.e., known to us all as, 'The Fall of Man'. Yet biology and history know nothing of such a calamity. Of man's rise, they both have had much to tell us, but of his fall, they have never spoken.

What then was this original sin? Metaphysically, it was the revolt of the Many against the One, i.e. to prefer a personal, independent existence in time, to a life hidden with God in eternity. Somehow, it became possible for human souls to embark upon separate lives, to exchange a blessed unity for the pursuit of private aims, i.e. to choose 'Becoming' on our own account, rather than 'Being', remaining with the One; i.e. to prefer a progressive to a static state. The essence of religion appears to be recognition of the One. Question: "What does the Lord require of thee?" Answer: "To remember the One."

Christianity interpreted, requires deliverance from the self, from the tyranny of the will-to-live. To turn against the will-to-live, to deny it, is the only absolute good, the only radical cure for the disease of life. However, a revolt against the will-to-live, should it prove successful, must lead to the extinction of all life, to final nothingness, more attractively expressed as union with God, as the final, desirable state. This interpretation turns its back on time, and declares for eternity, in which all distinctions vanish, and the last dew-drop slips into the shining sea. Life, then, is a huge mistake. The best is never to have been born; the second best, to die. Christianity has become committed to the conclusion that, in deliverance from our Earthly lot, and return to our former state, lies our only hope. Or if not, is Christianity then, anything more than an ethical gospel, the religion of philanthropy? One more question should be faced and answered. "What are we to understand by the term, "eternal life", of which philosophy and religion speak?" 'Heaven', 'eternity' and 'union with God' – are these phrases synonymous with 'the extinction of individual existence'? It is well to bear in mind that this eternal life will not restore us to our lost friends. It will neither reunite lovers parted by death, nor provide any compensation for the cruelties and injustices that men have endured.

Crucially, the simple question to which people desire an answer is: "Do the dead exist?" If there is no individual life beyond the grave, then the followers of Christianity have been sadly deceived, and its history is the greatest deception ever practised upon suffering humanity. When St. Paul said, "O death, where is thy sting?" or, "O grave, where is thy victory?" was he just indulging in a false and windy rhetoric?

Some theologians believe that the confirmation of a belief in a future life, is undesirable. They are mistaken. How long would

Christianity survive the extinction of this supporting pillar of belief? Christianity would then become, 'Morality touched with emotion', a gentle humanitarianism, which Dostoyevsky held to be the form of atheism most to be dreaded – the greatest anti-religious force in Europe. Men will no longer distress themselves to save their souls, when, apart from the present, they have no souls to save. Nor will it survive long if it proposes to make, by resignation, of deliverance from the World, of abstention from its natural activities, and by withdrawal and retreat, the end to be achieved. "There is no gain in shutting out the World, though it be with walls of righteousness." [Maeterlinck]

Do we all then need a more heroic religion? Definitions of God are not so much perilous as they are insane. Also, there is no value in a belief, which fails to move us. A wise man holds by the faith that provides for him the strongest incentive for living, and raises his highest powers. Blake said that all deities reside in the human breast, to which Spinoza added that a community of triangles would worship a triangular God. Hence, your God is your ideal. The architect is present in the building, but not a trace of him is visually present in its structure. But this sort of argument was neither advanced by Jesus, nor found in the New Testament. The God of love does not reside in 'the palace built for him by the metaphysicians.'

Can man take an interest in a God, who is uninterested in him? Man asks for a helper and it is the existence of an ever-present help in time of trouble that is in doubt. Conscious man prostrates himself before an unconscious God, unaware of the worship. What kind of ridiculous piety is this?

"You can be sure of God, though not sure of the argument", said Jeremy Taylor, i.e. experience and faith dispense with proof. The discoveries of goodness, poetry, beauty, music, religion and morals are man's discoveries. This implies that in the soul itself, there resides a divine principle, of which these are the fruits. The power of religion to confer happiness, to give peace, has abundant testimony in its favour.

Yet we may be sure that there are such things as obsolete and superannuated ideas, which have served their time, and are no longer useful. For example: to quarrel with the conditions of existence; to crucify yourself; to look upon resignation as the key to religion; to believe that God, or man, must be held to blame for the human situation; and to believe that 'The Fall of Man' was the great, original catastrophe. What can be substituted? Are there any alternatives? We could call 'The Fall of Man' his coming of age. It could be regarded as the time at which a World of finite creatures came into being. Then we might look at ourselves with greater interest, respect and with less pity. If we could replace the idea of a 'lost paradise' with that of the World as a family estate, left continuously to a resolute company of men, rather than to human beings loitering forever through fields of asphodel. Would this be an impious, or dangerous, thought? "Why stand we here", said Blake, "trembling around, calling on God for help, and not ourselves, in whom God dwells?"

We must do our best, and yet never expect too much either of ourselves, or of our fellow creatures. "What assurance have we of final victory?" But soldiers are not those who require to be assured of it, before taking the field. We must build on what we know and have, making of human experience and history a foundation for our efforts and ideals. All that the Earth provides, we must like – nothing is superfluous, nothing is to be rejected. And if it is not our positive duty to give value to the ideas in which we believe, to give them enduring forms, to ensure their acceptance, for the good of future generations, to fight for them, "to adorn our Sparta" then, if this is not our duty, will we ever know what is?

Turning now from the professors of knowledge (ethics) to the professors of conduct (morals), who tell us what we should do and why. These have dealt more often in censure rather than praise. They have prescribed a rigorous discipline for themselves and believe that their fellows are, at least, equally in need of it. Yet to find a foundation for morality is hard. Nevertheless, philosophers agree that the conduct of men is a matter of supreme consequence. Good behaviour is the cement of society. There is no safety, or order, in the World without it. But how is this behaviour to be maintained? On what principle can laws be enacted? The question is whether or not to profess ethics without a basis, "If the deity does not exist, then only the ill-disposed can be said to reason, the good are without sense." If what happens in the World, is really to be what physical science takes it for, then we can't talk the language of ethics and must jettison conduct. Outside of religion, no firm basis for morals can be found. But there still remain the ethical idealists. They believe that if human society is to be preserved from destruction, then there is a crying need for morals. "Lest men might do as they pleased, and so the World become a total wreck". The stability of society is their one and only concern. Nietzche ridiculed the English shallow-pates, who, when they had abandoned the Christian God, illogically retained Christian morality. But what were they to do, if they could find no other religion? To the question, "Why not?" to a life of revelry and sensuous delights, the ethical idealists became exasperated – "Pleasure is empty", say the Puritans, "it passes away." Ah yes, but the ascetic as well as the reveller goes, and who has the better of the bargain?

"Everyone admits," wrote Machiavelli, "how praiseworthy it is in princes to keep faith, live with integrity and not with craft. But great princes have held good faith of little account, and have circumvented the intellect of men by craft, and, in the end, have overcome those who have placed reliance on their word." Schiller went a step further, "Not a single example can be shown of a people where a high level and a wide universality of aesthetic culture went hand in hand with political freedom and civic virtue, or where beautiful manners went with good morals, or polished behaviour with truth." And so we see that we remain in the region of the contraries, of conflicting ideals, in which the World is born of the two opposites.

Ethics never lifts its eyes from the present scene; it is earthbound and thinks only of the prosperity and security of our daily lives. Regard for rule, which is ethics, and regard for the person, which is religion, are widely separated and often have irreconcilable interests. Supposedly, religion is based upon affection for humanity. It extends hope, consolation, pity and encouragement for suffering mortals. For religion, man's destiny is the supreme issue. But the 'categorical imperative' (ethics) is it kind? If not, then it is neither human nor divine. "Act so that your action can be universalised, i.e. can apply to all men in a similar situation." Yes, very exalted, and very useless; because in this vexing World, situations are invariably unique. Thus the 'categorical imperative' needs to be banished to an uninhabited island, where it can contemplate its own perfection.

Isn't it curious that morality never intrudes into our dreams? Neither does it make life worth living, or shed over it a beam of cheerfulness. "To be virtuous is to take pleasure in noble actions." Let the moralists solve the problem of: "How is goodness to be made the object of passionate desire, as attractive as fame, success, or even adventure?" In the same way that science inspires men to discover truth, if they could devise a morality that had the power to charm, then they would win most heads. Our reformers might do us a great service by explaining why a diet of milk and water does not appear to suit the human race, and only the lives of dare-devils, of buccaneers and of smugglers, captivate youthful souls. Why should the devil have all the best lines and tunes? "He had too much spirit to be a scholar." Must we add another to the commandments, "Thou shalt not have high spirits."

We have heard of the values of repression, renunciation and resignation, but how dispiriting they are as a panacea for one's ills! We are in need of more rather than less life. Why should we refuse to admit the infinite complexity and the innumerable windows through which the soul may view the astonishing landscape? Heaven save us from the blindness of single vision; from the philosopher's confined to the intellectual; the naturalist's to the physical; the moralist's to the ethical and the artist's to the aesthetic, view. If you choose to be an anchorite, then you cannot be a statesman. Once again, contradictions swarm in the very air we breathe.

There is no difference between kindliness and what is called virtue. Practical kindness is inseparable from virtue. But for the impulse towards kindness, already seated in human hearts, the talkers have little to say. The situation is similar for justice. If men cannot find justice in the courts of heaven, then they will not be persuaded to accept God as a judge. And an unjust God has nothing divine about him.

Ideas may be the most mysterious things in a mysterious World. Men have been convinced that science could save us (and still it might!), or universal suffrage would save us, or education for everyone would save us. Now universal peace will save us. During the middle ages, men believed in God, in themselves as sinful, and so in need of salvation. They never supposed that the World could be saved by any human efforts. They put their trust in their Creator and in a better World to come. Then the Renaissance arrived with a new and captivating bundle of ideas that exalted the European mind to an ecstasy of delight. The previous ideas seemed amazingly crude and mistaken. How unforeseen and startling were the alterations in opinion, how strange these secular revolutions. What brought this about? No change of any kind in the natural World. The change actually and astonishingly took place in the inner World of the mind, and/or heart, of humanity. We talk of the origins of cultures and of civilisations, but where have new, happy, or even misleading thoughts, their origins? The origin of ideas is perplexing. They tend to be sudden, beyond prediction, have a life of their own, independent of space and time, and come and go as they please. They are living and powerful entities. Some are short term, others last for a thousand years. They flourish according to their nature, in one soil, or climate, and droop in another. They are the vegetation of the mental World.

A fixed idea has great advantages. Our minds are at rest, and we are under neither necessity to defend it, nor to consider further evidence on the matter. But as Nietzche said, "When a fixed idea arises, a great ass makes its appearance."

A concept is an image, or picture, by which we try to make things clearer to ourselves, i.e. to understand them better. They are postulates and have value in science. However, we must not trust them for too long, or too completely. When scientific hypotheses cease to keep in step with observed facts, they are discharged ruthlessly. Similarly, we may ask whether or not a number of ethical concepts are in need of revision. When religions denounced the World of the flesh and the devil, and ethics set forth to wear down the will-to-live, were they not involved in fixations of thought, whose day was done, and in need of other and more encouraging concepts? We should look to exchange the thought that narrows and restricts for that which enlarges and stimulates the mind.

The recurring moods of the soul, we have seen, are of the contraries, the night that contradicts and yet is followed by the day. But what indeed is truth, what is goodness and what is beauty? Perhaps these are the things we need to discover. Who has defined them for us properly? The soul of man is not yet awake, not by thousands of years. His ethics and religions are no more than stammering efforts to speak an unknown language. They do reflect some common experience, but the expression of it is lacking. Yet it is possible to accept Hegel's (or Confucian?) advice, "Be a person, and treat others as persons, or even better, be a gentleman." There are not many better formulas. And if we ask, "How do we order our lives?" The answer is, "Exactly as our predecessors have done." Never regard this as final, but as provisional, until we can improve on it. In creation is perpetual and unfailing delight. Every man is bent on some sort of creation. Nature revels in it. Even the laws of nature are not static. Is it absurd to suppose that we are far from knowing the true nature of truth, of beauty and of goodness? Whatever our attachment to reason, let us remember that the secret of the World's everlasting interest lies precisely here, that we cannot explain it, and can never know what is going to happen next. This is the source of our abiding hope and never dying expectation.

Our Philosophy: What is undeniable? Professor M^c.Taggart took for his foundation, not the famous, "I think, therefore I am", of Descartes, but a more general proposition, "Something exists". This something does include ourselves, at least momentarily. To exist, if you reflect about it, appears to be the most natural state, and yet the most puzzling. Our awareness of the situation, i.e. our conscious life, first emerges as a distinction we draw between ourselves and our surroundings. "Here am 'I'", each of us says, "and over there is something else." "'I' and 'not-me'", is the distinction between subject and object and marks our first mental step. Some animals, we discover, are like ourselves in a number of ways, and we establish communication with them of one kind and another. We remember that the true-blue philosophers have no eye for this situation. They are concerned with a professional passion for the invisible, which does not trouble others in the least, i.e. the Absolute, in which all the various objects are fundamentally a unity. What clearness, finality, perfection and mental comfort there is in a circle, or of its very idea. So there is a similar, clearer finality and perfection in the idea of the One, the Whole and the all-containing Absolute. The peace that the idea provides is bound up with 'the Whole' as a closed system. But how do they know all this?

   Please note a characteristic of the human mind. Why do we prefer to think in this way, to go behind and deny the plain evidence of our senses that there are numerous and very different things, in favour of a doctrine that they are all, ultimately, one and the same? Reason opposes the testimony of the senses, rejecting the distinct information they give. In short, seeing is not believing. But by this means we save ourselves trouble by economy of thought, bringing different things under the same category and by pigeon-holing them we attain a sense of tranquillity and security. We also open up the possibility of bringing unusual, eccentric and hazardous things under our control, and of rising superior to our circumstances.

Another peculiarity of the human intellect is its desire to see things clearly and distinctly so that there is no mistaking what they are. The terms we apply here are all associated with sight. We say, "I see that", "How lucid", or "As clear as daylight". Conversely, in terms of argument, darkness is depressing and distasteful, and so corresponds to the unintelligible. "How obscure", we say, or, "We have to grope for his meaning", or, "He is blind to that view of the matter".

Regarding the origin of our universe (or, if there are other universes, out of any relation with ours, then they can be of no particular concern for us) modern physics, leaning upon the laws of entropy, asserts that the World/universe must have had a beginning. "The scheme of physics, as it has stood for the last three quarters of a century, postulates a date at which either the entities of the universe were created in a high state of organisation, or pre-existing entities were endowed with that organisation, which they have been squandering ever since. Moreover, this organisation is admittedly the antithesis of chance. It is something that could not have occurred fortuitously. [Sir Arthur Eddington]

Could it all have arisen without a cause, out of a previous nothing? But nothing can come from nothing, so we think. And it simply cannot be believed that it arose all at once, just like it is at present. We could suggest that the World never had a beginning, it was always there, in some form of existence and can never go out of existence, or we may believe that it was created by a supreme external power, which existed before the World/universe, and could have brought it into being. If an unthinking energy produced our World, then no explanation of good and evil is required. Great issues depend upon our choice of an answer to this metaphysical problem, which concerns the theologian as much as the philosopher. However, there is a difference:-

The philosopher does not consider himself called upon to assign any particular state, or dignity, to the human race, to regard it in any sense as a separate kingdom, or state, within a greater. For him, human beings are merely things, more curious perhaps, but without any privileged rank, or position, over stones, flowers or stars. He is just at a loss to explain how and why all the separate, dissimilar things arose out of the One. On the other hand, the theologian has more serious matters to consider – two in particular. He desires to maintain the absolute perfection of the One, of God the Creator, who, as he holds, made the World, and to account, at the same time, for the evils and imperfections present in his creation; and preserving, moreover, the supreme unity of God, to provide a separate status for man, an independent existence and will, which confer upon him responsibility for his actions, without which he becomes a merest non-entity, with no firm standing in the World than a wave of the sea, or a grain of desert sand. If God is all in all, then man is nothing. If man be, in any sense, an independent creature, his own master, who can go his own way, then God has lost control of his World. Glorify the Whole and the parts correspondingly lose their importance and significance. Exalt the parts and the majesty of the Whole is diminished. The philosopher is free from this foregoing, the theologian's anxiety. But with their differing dilemmas, neither religion, nor philosophy, has grappled successfully.

We have, let us suppose for the moment, a unity. Accepting the doctrine that everything derived originally from one source, and whatever its nature, we are involved in metaphysics, i.e. into an enquiry that goes beyond physics. How did it come to give birth to its multitudinous and very dissimilar products? This is the vexatious puzzle of the One and the Many. From the idea of a divine, creative intelligence to that of a vortex of material particles, out of whose continual clashing, accidental and interminable, there arose the outstanding texture, of which, we ourselves are the most astonishing part. Our bodies, our minds and the external World – all are knit up in the same tapestry. This monistic doctrine meets great difficulties. The safest way is to weave both opinions and say that Being is the Many and One, and that it is controlled by Love and Hate. Somehow the One became the Many, and so gave rise to a World that, otherwise, would not have come into existence.

However far we travel into the dark backward, and abysm of time, we travel to explain the present. We must suppose the past was of such a kind as to render the present possible. If we hold by the notion of causation at all, the past necessarily contained the possibility of the present. The One must itself release its powers and provide the opposing principle, the resisting energy. Consider a motionless and calm lake among the hills, exhibiting no sign of strength, yet this can give rise to a foaming torrent of leaping, plunging waters, so we may think of the unmoving and perfect One, transposed by its own act into the turbulent Many, the angry contending surges of a World at war.

If we have satisfied ourselves that the World is a physical one, through and through, made up of material particles, and can trace all its varieties, physical and mental, to combinations of these particles, or atoms, we still have to account for the particles and for the void in which they float, for their origin, i.e. the problem of a first cause. If we begin with atoms, then obviously it took them a long time to arrange themselves into the World as we see it, and into the creatures it contains – a very long time. In this regard, miracles, perhaps, become not quite so remarkable, if we have millions upon millions of years to perform them. And we still have to begin with space and time, which, wherever they come from, when they got together, had some very heavy work before them, to construct the universe. However, it is necessary to begin with something somewhere, and if we pursue this line of investigation/explanation, we try to picture a gradual process of development, of evolution, from the original substance to the present state of things.

If our imagination fails before this conception, then we have mentioned alternative theories. But the World seems beyond our comprehension and yet, "The true logic for this World is the Calculus of Probabilities, the only mathematics for practical men", said Clark Maxwell. "Probability is the guide of life." But we must guard against Idealism and Materialism. Idealism is often no more than an inverted materialism and provides nothing better for man's spiritual welfare. We must not trust "Idealism", the wolf in sheep's clothing of the philosophic schools.

There seems no other way of creating a finite World save through the negation of the One of Being, and this, again, seems inconceivable, save as resistance to the One, and the conflict of each with all. We may think of the World as the awakening of the Many within the One. Yet, if the One gave birth to the Many, it ended by devouring its offspring. For the monistic doctrine, the Many are only the creatures of a day.

History begins with time – a story is the unfolding of events in time, and, for us, there is no penetrating into eternity. God negates himself, in order that there may be a World, and this negation, or sundering, is creation's dawn.

Following on from this rather unsatisfactory situation, we may say that no philosophic system, which begins with the One, or Absolute, has succeeded in discriminating among its emanations, or for providing for some (such as ourselves) as against others, of any enduring value, or significance.

<u>Pluralism:</u> As a more promising route for beginning our philosophical journey with matters nearer at hand, and as we know them, let us take council with the pluralists, the friends, or adherents, of the Many. The doctrine of the One is beyond the pluralists scrutiny, and so a profitless discourse. The Many (the appearances) are in possession of the visible field, and possession is nine tenths of the law. However they arrived on the scene, the appearances did, at least, appear, which is something. Let us begin then, the pluralists advise, with 'The Furniture of the Earth, and The Choir of Heaven.'

One pluralist philosopher of the first rank was Leibniz, the chief protagonist of the pluralists' way of thinking. Although born in 1646, nearly three hundred years ago, his scientific acumen and prescience enabled him to foresee, and even in a measure anticipate, many conclusions arrived at by the most recent science.

The World may be best understood as consisting of an infinite variety of living and active beings, monads, as he called them, each a separate and distinct centre of energy. The monads are of many grades and levels; the whole forming a staircase of living creatures. The World is not a machine. Everything in it is force, life, thought and desire. Each monad seeks the fulfilment of its own peculiar needs. The World, in brief – a noble thought, and at least worthy of belief – is a living society. What light does this throw upon our immediate experience? It reports that energy is operative throughout the length and breadth of the World, which is, indeed, a texture of energies. It reports that nature exhibits both order and disorder, sympathies and antipathies, purposes and cross-purposes, i.e. is fissured by such opposites as are to be found in human society and within ourselves. These contrary forces present a mystery to those who believe in the One, an enigma utterly beyond resolution. Perhaps a similar state of contrary forces prevails throughout the whole structure. Suppose the World's existing patterns are the outcome of striving selves. Suppose further that the division we make between animate and inanimate is a needless dichotomy and that the constituent atoms themselves, charged with vital energy, are each living and spiritual in their essential nature. Life, as we know, proceeds only from previous life, but where is the dividing line to be drawn, as, for example, in the case of the viruses? So pervasive and ubiquitous is the will-to-live that it exists, even in what to us, appears to be inanimate nature. A modern, physiological view maintains that consciousness, however primitive, is primary and has grown to narrower, more dominating, higher levels within the organism, i.e. throughout the World mind controls matter, and not *vice-versa*. Assume that where there is life, there is intelligence, which all living things, in some elementary form, display. If only we adduce probabilities, as likely as any other, then that ought to be enough for us. Why not admit that the World is a living, rational being, since it produces animate and rational entities? Nature hasn't given birth to life – she is life. The World is not the home of life, only because it is itself alive. And the mind develops only in the co-operations and frictions of society.

However, we must still find a meeting place for the individual monads, a ground for their interaction. They cannot be wholly unrelated and solitary wanderers in the boundless void. If the One cannot produce a World, then the Many are equally powerless without the One. Hegel said that finite existences can only be really individual and differentiated in proportion as they are united between themselves in a closer unity. For example: the organs of a human body are contained in a closer unity than the stones in a heap, and, at the same time, these organs have each a more individual nature, than have these self-same stones.

Additionally, we may be sure that our destiny is the World's destiny, and that our journey is its journey; nothing less is to be believed. The World everywhere shows purpose and the supreme purpose of the World at least includes and provides a scene, or realm, of purposes woven by the individual selves, but the supreme purpose itself, and the history of the World, are not in our hands.

We must revise and enlarge our categories of thought, for the logic of yesterday will not serve us today and forever. We are deceived if we imagine that the mind, which has had a long history, has no more to say, or that the World, whose history is as long, has wound up its affairs. There is much to come. Modern sciences have made the World appear to be more and more an open one, i.e. as a World not closed, but pointing beyond itself. "We could believe that the World is wider and larger than the wisest of even philosophers have ever conceived. Let us try to think imperially, for the more magnificent our thoughts, the nearer the truth they may well be."

The Concept of Space-Time, and Here and Now. Since 1900, certain aspects of nature, associated with the senses, have forced themselves upon the attention of physicists and mathematicians, so that they have had to consider the most obstinate of our metaphysical problems, namely the great twin mysteries of the natures of time and space. These must somehow be incorporated into the account of physics, into its description of the extensions, durations, motions and boundaries of the external World. Thus we suppose ourselves to have come to closer quarter with these concepts and their huge significance in the grand scheme of things. Now they are seen to be the guardians of all the mysteries.

But what can we say about them? We speak of days, nights, months and years, but what is it that we so divide? We speak continually of 'Here' and 'Now', but where is 'Here', which goes about with us wherever we go, and when is 'Now', which is always slipping away to make way for another 'Now'? Do we realise that if there were no spectators of the moving scene of nature, then there would be no 'Heres' and no 'Nows'? 'Here' is here for someone; 'Now' is now for someone. Nature, which is everywhere at once, has no 'Heres' and no 'Nows'. For us, space and time appear to contain all things:

everything lies within space, and everything happens within time. There they are, perpetually present; the terrifying apparition of time, never beginning and never ending, "the moving image of eternity"; and that other, no less terrifying spectre, the abyss of space. Remove everything in thought, and all the worlds, so that there remains the vast void, which refuses to go. Time and space provide the setting for our little lives, and in this horizonless expanse, the whole of the history of mankind shrivels into nothingness, becomes a mere flicker, or a momentary flash of lightning, in an unfathomable night.

And yet, how serenely our Earth and Moon glide silently together, without a ripple, through the uncharted gulf. In the divine stillness of that limitless ocean, they are at home. An ocean of what? Of nothing, it seems, nothing at all. How far does this emptiness extend, through which our universe journeys, and whither can we suppose it to be journeying?

We can see that time and space are unlike anything else, with which we have any acquaintance. There is nothing with which to compare them. But we can say with confidence that things themselves, in any sense of the World, they cannot be. We can imagine space, which contains no bodies. Time, too, without events – sometimes called 'duration' – we can indeed imagine; yet of empty, eventless time, we could not be conscious. Of neither space, nor time, do our senses give us the slightest information. Travelling fast, or slow, we don't approach the terminus of either; and if time is flowing, then it is flowing without anything that flows. How can the insubstantial come into contact with, or have any relation with, the substantial objects that surround us? How came material things to enter this immaterial framework?

The same insuperable problem meets us when we try to understand how thought can lay hold on substance. For the World of our understanding and thoughts, and the World of solid things, are like two rivers, which flow side by side, yet seemingly never meet.

"Neither we, nor anyone else", declared Kant, "can explain how this harmony between thought and things came about; as if nature had been arranged expressly to suit our purposes of comprehension". By some kind of natural magic, the objects seen by the eye, the sounds heard by the ear, became those ghostly, yet real things, we call ideas. Somehow there exists, between the mind and the external World, a connection that baffles the philosophers.

Considering further, we realise that space and time appear to have certain resemblances and most interesting differences. Space possesses the three dimensions of length, breadth and height. Everywhere in space, three ways meet. And time has, for us, though not for nature, three phases, or successive dimensions; past, present and future. The dimensions of space are intimate; they are simultaneous and never found apart, while those of time, on the other hand, are never found together. When the future puts in an appearance to become the present, the former present vanishes into the past. Different from space, which for us is stationary, time seems to move in one, or other, direction.

There is also a very notable peculiarity of time – its irreversibility. There is no going back in time, no undoing of what has once been done. Time alters everything, both in the organic and inorganic Worlds. Change is the supreme, fundamental feature, the terrible, unceasing restlessness; the continued 'Becoming', which is at the root of all our anxieties and woes. We cry out for peace, for rest, for a cessation of this perpetual and distressing flux, for the eternity of changeless 'Being'; the goal of the mystics craving. But the World, ceaselessly in movement, knows nothing of such a World, or such a state. Time and change are the World's masters. Stars, mountains, seas and continents bow themselves before his omnipotent, serene majesty, Time.

Now, we know that the available energy is continually decreasing (the 2nd law of Thermodynamics) and so we have a direction post, which points one way only. It points to a downward slope into the gulf of a final and irremediable stagnation. Thus, time presents an inexorable countenance. A profoundly significant something is taking place, of which it is the index, with which human destiny is inseparably associated.

Let us mention two, among the many, theories of time. The first is the theory of absolute time, something that exists quite apart from us, and from the events that take place in it, something independent of all other things, which flows steadily along and which has moments, to which events, when they occur, can be assigned. Most philosophers reject absolute time. Hume and Berkeley held that space was merely the manner in which objects exist with an absence of resistance. So, too, thinkers like Kant and Leibniz, held that, secondly, time has no independent existence, and was merely the relationship between phenomena, or events. Further, both space and time were subjective, which make experience possible for us; however, of appearances only, and not of the reality that underlies them. Neither is real, and both are mental structures. Yet time is something deeper than the mere relationship of events to each other, i.e. in our way of seeing them. And we need to bear in mind that time, in itself, though often confused with our awareness of time, plays a part of its own in the universe.

How can physics, in any manner, grapple with aspects of nature, which are clearly not physical, and which are wholly insubstantial? Neither space, nor time, has any ingredients. Where in time, or space, do we fix our point of departure and in what unit, in either case, do we propose to apply? Yet space and time appear to have some superficial resemblances, and clearly are somehow associated with each other. We estimate space by the passing of time, so that they are already associated. But unlike space, for which we have no inner sense, we appreciate time in two ways. There is an inner, or private, time and an outer, or public time. The mind has its own sense of the passage of time depending on our circumstances. But we substitute for this true time, another, which is used by astronomers, due to the grand intrusion of space. Thus, we imagine an outer time, which science looks upon as measurable, i.e. clock time. Between these two times, however, some correspondence does appear to exist, as has been shown by hypnotism. Thus, the sidereal heavens, the atom and the mind, all appear to have time scales of their own. We may well have to add a 'biological' time, which governs the growth and activities of the living organism – but this tends to be too variable, depending on conditions.

Space, we gather, is composed of electromagnetic fields (of the heavenly bodies) and it is of these fields, or what they contain, and not of space itself, of which physics is invariably speaking.

If we ask about time, then this is measured by adopting the speed of light, as a limiting, or maximum, velocity, to which no acceleration can be given. In this way, physics obtains a measuring rod for time (speciously objectified) but its true nature is thereby adroitly eluded and ignored. If a faster messenger than light were admitted to be possible, let us suppose an instantaneous intuition, an observer, so equipped, might become aware of an event before, from the scientific point of view, it had happened, i.e. before the scientific messenger, the light signal, reached him with the news that the event had taken place. Thus, we could see the peculiar paradoxes with which Relativity theory is beset – the local times that replace simultaneity and the bulge, or curvature, of space-time, which consists of nothing, and so is insubstantial. These paradoxes are due to the fact that modern physics is not dealing with space and time at all, but solely with things masquerading in their place/room. "It is impossible to meditate on time and the mystery of the creative passage of nature, without generating within yourself an overwhelming emotion about the limitations of human intelligence." [Whitehead]

Science (physics mainly) has always proceeded in the daring, magnificent assumption that nature was intelligible, that it could be comprehended. To believe this, we need to believe in the uniformity of nature, and believe that what she did yesterday, she could do today and forever. It may be much nearer the truth to say that science has deepened all the old mysteries, making more marvellous, what was already marvellous, leaving us, and her own adventurous spirit, dumbfounded. And, in the end, though in herself so glorious a witness to human powers, just let us try to be aware of what science has actually omitted from the account.

There are truths of many kinds, of the senses, of inner and outer experience, of the heart as well as of understanding. And truth, of any and every kind, derives its sole value and significance from its relation to ourselves, to human life and destiny. Nature has no values. Only when sentient creatures appear, do values also. If we set values and their appreciation aside, in effect, we set everything aside and reduce the World to a whirlpool of nonsense.

As the World consists of selves, we are at once driven to regard their interests and values, as supreme, and above all mere events. The only existent that includes all others is consciousness; the appanage (special support) of the self. The attempt to derive the self from atoms and the void, from space and time and to deny it any constructive role in the system of nature, has not failed for lack of unceasing and desperate effort, but rather because we cannot explain the self in terms of the not-self.

Future philosophers will allow to the self its unique status, its standing as a factor, a primary and organising factor, in the World as a whole. This will reinstate personality in its true place in the World, and leave room for its expansion. Both the World and man have a history. They had a past and will have a future. No doubt that future will contain no fewer unpredictable and surprising events.

<u>The Web of Life and Ourselves.</u> "The most irrational theory of all is that elements without intelligence should produce intelligence", said Plotinus.

Good and evil are not found unalloyed, or in isolation, but inter-wrought in a pattern, or network, which is the World, and without which no World could be. For the illogicality and accidents of life, its casual encounters, its hazards, mischances, eccentricities and humours, some other explanation is required. The pluralistic model finds in these, no invincible difficulties, since although the Many seek good and only good, evil, as well as good, is to be expected in the World of their making, in their diverse desires and conflicting ideals. The World then becomes less a comedy than a tragedy: "a comedy to the intellect, a tragedy to the heart." If, now, we prefer this model and accept the World as a process, and a growing, or 'Becoming', how shall we describe those agencies to whose activities it owes its confused and complicated character? There are self-conscious entities like ourselves, the sensitive and intelligent higher animals, others with dim consciousness like the plants, and finally, below the plants, we reach entities to whom it seems altogether absurd to ascribe individual existence in, or for, themselves, in any sense; the elements and minute/atomic components, which are, by comparison with living things, vast in quantity. Yet mind does more than matter can. And everywhere the presence of energy argues for the presence of life, and the presence of life argues for the presence of will, and, at least, nascent intelligence. The thing, whose life is patent to sense, is made up of things that patently don't live, but nonetheless confer upon their resultant total, wonderful powers toward living (emergent properties through increased complexity, e.g. consciousness).

However, it is no longer forbidden for us to think of nature as a grand society, a hierarchy, and to say that everywhere mind acts, not upon dead matter, but, at all times, directly upon mind.

Consider the famous affair of causation. Habitually, we trace events to their causes. The idea of cause is the great central pillar, not only of scientific thought, but of all thought. Nature's order and uniformity are preserved by statistical laws. A high degree of probability/ expectation should meet all our requirements. Individual entities are metaphysical units, as monads, each in some degree a self, or soul, and views the World as their scene of interaction. A continuity of some kind, could we follow it, runs through the whole of creation, and is without doubt a spiritual one. That aspect of the World that includes conscious thought, will, meaning and purposes, cannot now be explained, or even coherently imagined, in any physical terms at all. Thinking, remembering, believing, feeling and willing, are not electromagnetic, or special, processes. We may conclude then, that mind is ultimate, and that the World system comprises a manifestation of many minds (and mind includes feelings, desires and wills, as well as intellect). Mind did not appear first in man, though it was there that we had certain knowledge of it. Body, or organism, CAN be identified with the individual, and not just as that individual's representative in the material World.

Personality, in its final analysis, is simply will, or cause. However, the body, or organism, associated with the individual self, through which its inner life is manifested, is, in the common World of all existences, at once its means of communication with other selves, and its protection against the bewildering extent and multiplicity of their activities. The body is thus a kind of sorting place, or telephone exchange, "Nature must be adjusted to the dimensions of the human animal and human consciousness." Hence we may think of the body as a screen, or resistance coil, which diminishes the pressure of these activities, or lowers the tension to the point at which they can, in some degree, be supported and apprehended, i.e. by our bodies, the World is scaled down, or reduced, to the measure of our own powers. Within its immensity, we can keep our feet, and hold our own. We can select and order our experiences. As a result, the self is brought by the body into simpler and working relations with the rest of the World; it becomes provided also with a spiritual perspective. And so the World of Space and Time resembles an artist's picture, in which the landscape of reality is reduced and separated from the whole, and framed for our contemplation. [All this is speculative, yet it does seem reasonable. However, practical philosophers, no doubt, would have us abandon speculation, and go and cultivate our gardens.]

We are, no doubt, of some trifling importance to ourselves, but to attach any importance, or significance, to mankind is difficult. We want to think nobly of ourselves, but the ship of life is small and the sea of circumstances so wide that we become discouraged. And Mother-Nature does neither hasten to her children's material, or spiritual, assistance, nor provide praise and encouragement.

Consider how small a part of Earth's surface is fit for human habitation. How little of its land provides a salubrious climate, or easy ways of life for its inhabitants. Consider too, inclement seasons, droughts and floods, wild beasts and noxious insects, fires and pestilences, idiocy and mania, abnormalities and accidents, etc. Mankind has a harsh and hard row to hoe. Lower animals seem better equipped, with talents suited to their life conditions, than we. Consider also, the cruelties, the surly, bitter tempers, the fault-finding and vituperation, the superstition and foolery, the intrigues, deceptions, rivalries and envies, swindling and villainy, the petty scandals, the absurd pursuits and ambitions, and worst of all, perhaps, the outrageous injustices. Our moralists and satirists have a broad and easy target for their denunciations and derision. It seems that the human race was born under a very unlucky star!

So with what can we counter these discouraging features? – Only our contemptible selves. Personality comes first. Something of celestial origin [astrology?] may be found and it is here that the main issue of human destiny lies in the balance.

But what of the self? – Does it exist? Experts and great authorities deny and dispose of us, and incidentally, of themselves. The worst that psychology can do is to rob the soul of its worth. Leibniz wrote that a soul may have a body composed of parts, each of which has a soul of its own, but the soul of the whole is not composed of the souls of its parts. Thus, the parts will never enable you, however deeply studied, to understand the whole. Every animal, moreover, like ourselves, acts teleologically, i.e. with a purpose in its doings. It adjusts itself, and adapts to the future. The soul provides, not receives, the unity. That 'I' should be here now, in this region of time, seems beyond comprehension [But it isn't]. Similarly, that 'I' should belong to this World, or to a particular portion of it, who will make this clear? [But it can be done].

However, we may say that the self is the only point of departure for any kind of enquiry. Apart from a self, we cannot find a mind, and apart from mind, there is no such thing as consciousness. When we speak of experience, we can only mean the experience of a self, for there is no other. When we say that anything appears, we can only mean appearance to a subject (self). There is no perception of an object in the absence of a subject. A feeling of toothache is someone's feeling; a desire to eat, or drink, is someone's desire; the intention to take a walk, is someone's intention. One and all, these are activities of a self.

No-one will say that there is no such thing as feeling. Yet there is NO such thing, except in the experience of a sentient subject. Emotions, too, are states of the self. If the self should perish, then its memories are lost forever. We act forwardly, but we know backwardly. Despite its stupendous immensity, the universe is not aware of 'me', or of itself. 'I' in my insignificance, am aware of myself, and of the World. This statement declares that 'you' and 'I' possess a supreme talent denied to the universe. 'We' are awake, as nothing else in creation is awake. The most enigmatical, indescribable and undeniable attribute of the self is its awareness. However can such an awakening, at all, or anywhere, come about?

Before dismissing the self, we should do well to ponder its aristocratic prerogative, which makes all else appear as a negligible cipher. From its lofty position, all the kingdoms of Earth and Heaven may be surveyed. For our part, we hold that neither intellect, nor imagination; neither science, nor logic, can explain how the advent of consciousness, i.e. the World's coming to a knowledge of itself, came about. Though surrounded by, and embedded in the World, this awareness, this unique appanage, or endowment, of the original self, marks its absolute separation from the rest of creation. It is 'I' myself, independently opposing myself to the 'not-self', affirming, and at the same time, resisting the whole, in my resolution to be, and to continue to be what I am, thinking and willing for myself; viewing myself and expressing myself from a standpoint not to be identified with any other, throughout the past, or present, history of the World, lonely and unrepeatable, it is this 'I', this breakwater, against which the waves of denial burst in vain.

There is then something in us, which nature has not given, for she had it not to give. Selfhood is not a contingent entity, but the representative of a metaphysical and necessary principle of the World, a part of its essential nature, a constituent of reality; nor without it, could the World have obtained a recognition, to full consummation, or true being. Experiencing selves were thus a necessity to legitimise the World. In a word, the self brings everything into view.

Consciousness from a material universe, apart from existing selves, is not possible, and that it could produce the power to create its own spectators, is also impossible.

It is the capacity of awareness, not the act, which is in question. How did this capacity come to birth? [Once again, it is an emergent property, due to the increased complexity of our brains that brings it about.]

How then, does the new story of creation run? Is it the old materialism in a new guise? In the beginning was Space-Time, whatever that may be, and Space-Time finding eternity, or half an eternity, heavy on its hands, said, "Let there be substantial things." And with the assistance of elements, electromagnetic energies, and the rest of its imaginary progeny, Space-Time produced the great galaxies, and the host of Heaven. There they were shining in the night sky. But then, after a lapse of infinite ages, it somehow dawned upon Space-Time that it had toiled in vain, its glorious works remained, alas, unseen, unknown, utterly unnoticed, unrecognised and unaccepted anywhere, throughout its imperial immensity. How disappointing, how intolerable a result, after so mighty and prolonged a labour. So grotesque a situation called for a further supreme effort, an effort, after untold exertions and experimental assays beyond enumeration, but finally successful. And so, conscious selves were evolved in the Space-Time laboratories. Under magical persuasions of Space-Time, they took notice of the World. It was given an audience.

Such is the new story of creation for philosophical children. We could despise life and hate man, but, "the powers of the mouth, the wisdom of the brow, the human comprehension of the eyes and the outstanding vitality of the creature", remain to confound us.

Men mistrust rationalism, which is much too simple-minded, to act as a guide, or interpreter, in this uncanny and incalculable World.

Retrospect. This World of ours is important, and although we may hope for a better, we need not look for a perfect World, either in the near, or distant, future, because it is imperfect of necessity. A World uniform and without variety, static and unchanging, could be no scene, or home, of life. Existence involves diversity and movement, and so, better and worse; light and dark and good and evil. It has its risks and upheavals and so is dangerous and will remain so. It involves the contraries, the ups and downs; the tidal rhythms, which preserve it from stagnation, and in whose absence, we could not be conscious of existence, or know ourselves to be alive. The good, too, is for growing and expanding entities – however they came to a knowledge of such a thing – the enemy of the best – for with what has already been attained, they cannot rest content, having hopes within them of a still better state, which imagined 'better' is the eternal critic of the present and actual. Such then, is our nature and destiny. Moreover, a perfect World is manifestly incompatible with myriads of beings, since each is in respect singular, or unique, and ever in search of its private and peculiar needs, entails loves and hates, collisions and oppositions. A World of any kind is, in a word, a synonym for what we have called 'the Many' and is the antithesis, or denial, of whatever perfection Unity, or 'the One' could be supposed to provide.

That 'the One' should be all in all, is to ask, as Heraclitus said, that the World, and we with it, should pass away. It is to express a preference for death over life. To escape the differences and the contraries, therefore, is, for us, impossible. They are our life blood. Life is movement, movement is life and movement is disturbance.

We arrived, too, at the conclusion that the <u>activities</u> (or souls, selves and monads) or energies that make up the World, limit and condition each other, and, what seem to us, material bodies, are the events that emerge from the interaction of these <u>activities</u>. 'Self'-existent matter must be ruled out as an impossible conception. To this conclusion, we add another, that the source of these <u>activities</u>, the souls, or monads, though in our restricted view they appear incessantly coming and going, arriving and departing, neither enter, not leave, the World, for it consists of them, and is, at the same time, the scene of operations, where infinite Being is progressively mirrored in Becoming. In these souls, or selves, we have the unique, unfathomable, constitutive and indispensable factors in the fundamental order. In these experiencing entities, and in them alone, can the system of nature find its recognition, and so without them, it has no true existence, dignity or worth. What is anything without beings to be aware of it? The answer can only be 'nothing'. In the absence of such beings, nature had neither risen to knowledge of herself, nor could the World know itself, or be known as a World.

We saw, too, that all manifested life is individual life, throughout the whole realm of nature, in its own manner and degree purposive. And the problem of change and permanence finds its solution in these individual souls, or selves. Like the streamers, or ribbons, of weed attached to a sea-girt rock, they sway to and fro in the tides of time, yet are rooted in the underlying and immutable reality. We must rid ourselves of the notion that the World is something outside ourselves, to which we belong accidentally. We are the World, in every fibre of our body and being, nerve and thought, as are all other souls, each a microcosm of that macrocosm.

Hippocrates, quoted by Leibniz, said, "Animals are not born, and do not die, and the things that we suppose to come into 'Being' merely appear and disappear." And we may, or may not, agree with this. They form the souls and monads, a vast society, a hierarchy of innumerable levels, of which in organic, and in inorganic nature, we see a part, as represented by the elements, the plants and the animals, an association the most intimate, an interlocked and interwoven confederacy. Thus the World is an arena, at once of conflicting and yet linked and united purposes, i.e. such as human society itself exhibits.

To resolve its age-long perplexity, we suggested that man has need to seek new concepts, to search profounder depths for the source of the contradictions that man deplores, which, nonetheless, the World displays. They are omnipresent, run through the whole extent of nature, and in the mind must be accepted and should be welcomed. For we seem driven to look for their origin at a deep level, in the very ground of Being itself. The old and simple antithesis, to which humanity has clung, upon which it has built its so many philosophies and religions, which it has pictured as a conflict between the powers of light and darkness; of good and evil; between Ormuz and

Ahriman, and between God and Satan – that old antithesis has failed. It will not serve to untie the Gordian knot, to account, either for the World's structure, or for the ironies of man's estate. The antagonistic principles we see at work, reside in Reality itself, and must there be resolved and reconciled. There we find also the attributes, equal and complementary principles, neither subordinate to the other, the two pillars of the World's structure. In their opposition lies the tension without which neither life nor consciousness exist, and in its absence, no World at all. But in the World of the two pillars, we may expect to find, as we do, pessimists and optimists, lovers of life and haters of it, lovers of activity and those of passivity, those of Becoming and those of Being. There should be room and verge enough for an infinite and invincible variety.

The Divine Arts. For some reason, nature, possibly because she has done all that she could, but probably for something more profound, having given us life, stayed her hand, with the unfortunate results that we see.

The best we have been able to do so far, is to create a dream World, a World of the imagination, superior in a number of ways to the World in which we live; much pleasanter and less substantial. The World of our acquaintance, 'the Many', or nature, is then, 'Being' externalised, our views of it; and 'Becoming' is, we might say, its revealed, or lighter side. For our own small share, we describe them as sleeping and waking states. On waking, a man leaves behind his anxieties, and enters 'Becoming', the turbulent arena of contending opposites. We may say that the realm of 'Being' is the World of reality; the World of 'Becoming', a World of appearances. It is in the latter state only, that experience is possible. Sir Thomas Browne said, "There is something in us that can be without us, and will be after us, though it is strange that it has neither history of what it was before us, nor cannot tell us, how it entered in us." Souls last as long as the World, and go from better to better", said Leibniz. What could be simpler, or reasonable, and more agreeable to thought, than the balanced rhythm of repose and activity that nature shows in her ebb and flow, in sleep and in waking, in death and life, in withdrawal and renewal? (But we may disagree with this.)

Conscious lives are our surface lives. Nature would have us undistracted, to attend only to this place and moment, the events of here and now. By our bodily senses, we are limited to the realm of 'Becoming'. But when we sink below the threshold of conscious and daily experiences, we can happily afford entrance to deeper moments by means of the fine arts. We become caught up into the abiding presence of, "That which was, and is, and ever shall be." And then this becomes, "We feel that we are greater than we know."

Thought is to space, as feeling is to time.

The arts of time (poetry and music) are intensive, not dimensional.

The arts of space (painting and sculpture) are for the intellect and stay the moment of 'Becoming', for our contemplation.

Reportedly, Beethoven said, "Music is the one incorporeal entrance into the higher World, which comprehends mankind, but which mankind cannot comprehend." The arts show us that our imperfect World contains harmonies and rhythms with which we find ourselves intimately in tune.

In the fine arts, man has travelled further from the animals, and nearer to the angels, than in any other of his enterprises, or accomplishments. Here, in some measure, he is a creator. Music and Poetry, Painting and Sculpture, on balance, have added considerably to the sum of human happiness. It is in works of art that nations have deposited their profoundest intuitions, and the ideas of their hearts. Fine art is frequently the key – with many nations there is no other – to the understanding of their wisdom, religion and custom. And the reason for this, is that they speak in the language of the soul, rather than of the intellect, in a Worldly language, understood by the World.

"There seems" said Aristotle, "to be a sort of relationship between the soul, on the one hand, and harmonies and rhythm on the other."

The inspired priestess, by whom the World is seen in the widest perspective, answers, "Your experience is real, but consult the God within you, and know that this real is not the whole of reality." Consider, for example, the occult chemistry by which the caterpillar transforms itself into a butterfly. Additionally, the astronomy of souls (astrology, which contains psychology?) is a more difficult science than that of the stars (a branch of physics).

In Plutarch's phrase, "The World is more good than bad." The soul, who can tell, to what heights of power and vision it may climb, to become fitted to choose for itself, the state and society as its natural and/or enduring habitation, which best meets its many requirements.

The Verdict. As Tolstoy said, "One can go on living when one is intoxicated by life, but as soon as one is sober, it is impossible NOT to see that it is all mere fraud . . . . I now see that if I did not kill myself, it was due to some dim consciousness of the invalidity of my thoughts. I (my reason) has acknowledged life to be unreasonable. But how can reason, which (for me) is the creator of life, and (in reality) the child of life, deny life? There is something wrong here."

Where lie the flaws? Not in his logic but in his unstated premises. The conclusion he draws rests upon three assumptions, i.e. that 1) we are in possession of all the relevant facts to form the judgement; 2) we know all we need to know to estimate the value of life and 3), last and most important, the included postulate that the skeleton, death, crowns, at the last, its emptiness, with appropriate derision. If any life beyond the present be denied, then we need go no further. If death be the gulf, to which the whole of creation moves, then, to what end, "all the sublime prerogatives of man?" Proclaim to men that, "Death is the only immortal", and religion receives its mortal wound. "If immortality be untrue," as Buckle wrote, "then it matters little whether anything else be true, or not." The World condemns itself.

Existence offers values only to the individual beings, who have a share in existence. If there be any good, and any beauty, then it can only be for them, and their perception of such things. If the valuators perish, then all values go with them into the everlasting night. We are offered, it seems, a sip from the cup of life, which is forever withdrawn. What kind of selfishness is this, which asks no more for one's self, than for all men and creatures ever born?

So whence come our present discontents? Probably from the collapse of the high-pitched expectations of a regenerated society. And the malady of our age is just the thought that nothing, or next-to-nothing, is, in truth, worth attempting, or achieving. "What gain to be summoned out of nothingness, into illusion and developed, only to aspire and to decay?" If, in the denial of my renewal of life beyond the grave, do we not then virtually deny all life's present values?" Tolstoy asked: "Is there any meaning in my life, which will not be destroyed by the inevitable death awaiting me?" The question requires an answer.

Only on some other postulate, then, can the case for existence be argued with success. We could say that the present life is incredible, a future credible. To be once born is wonderful. To have emerged from darkness and silence, and to be here today, is certainly incredible! 'I' find it easy to believe in miracles. For example, there are starry worlds in time and space; the pageant of life; the processes of reproduction and growth; the instincts of animals; the inventiveness of nature; the rising and the setting Sun; the affections and passions; the character of thought, of will, of consciousness; these singly and together plunge the human mind into profound amazement, to be in their midst. They are all miracles, piled upon miracles. 'I' see nothing but works of magic. If we look into the field of human faculty, into its still unexplored resources, into the testimony for the marvels that the submerged portion of our being reveals, then we shall not return with less amazement, but in a possible state of still greater stupefaction.

Don't talk of the credible and incredible, until we have looked further, from which, if well understood, a new vision of truth might arise. We are deceived indeed, if we fancy that our five senses exhaust the World. "The sensitive soul oversteps the conditions of time and space," wrote Hegel. Palatable, or unpalatable, we must accept whatever lies in the path of our destiny. The castle of our thought may need rebuilding from its foundations. For example, people talk glibly of telepathy, yet if extra-sensory perception alone, were established, the whole scheme of modern thought crumbles into ruin. It would be nothing short of a scientific revolution. "I would certainly NOT now say," wrote Bradley (1923), "that a future life must be taken as decidedly improbable." We cannot tell how many modes of existence there are, but we could imagine them to be very numerous. But we have to remind ourselves constantly, of the lock to which we do not possess the key, namely, the true character of time and our relations with it, which have never been determined, and upon which all hinges, i.e. the nature of time and change, of which we are wholly ignorant. On the other hand, we may be sure that what now exists in our experience, is consistent with all that anywhere exists, and cannot be rendered otiose, useless or irrelevant. If things, as they are, have not a feature in common with things as they will be, then we have no basis for thought at all regarding that future; but nature, we suspect, will remain the same. "A leap from one state to another, infinitely different state, could not be natural," said Leibniz. And before we can attain to that final harmony between the World and ourselves (to which we look forward as the consummation of existence), how much more we have to learn about them both! In our present life, we have acquired, at the most, the alphabet of this knowledge, and as for the World, of the modes of existence and happiness, which it may permit, we know less than nothing.

Immortality is a word that stands for the stability, or permanence, of that unique and precious quality we discern in the soul, which, if lost, leaves nothing worth preservation in the World. Since we are not to believe the World to be a misery-go-round, we may prefer to put our trust in the larger vision of poets (but not in the larger visions of scientists, or of philosophers!?). It is to their inextinguishable sympathy with humanity that they owe their understanding. The soul does not provide itself with a passport to an imaginary country, and cannot vibrate to a note unsounded in the World.

How simple then, is our duty – loyalty to life, to the ship's company and to ourselves, so that it may not be through our surrender that the great experiment of existence, whose issue remains in doubt, can come to an end in nothingness. "We must not obey," said Aristotle, "those who urge us, because we are human and mortal, to think only human and mortal thoughts; in so far as we may, we should practise immortality, and to omit no effort to live, in accordance, with the best that is in us." We should think that this singular race of indomitable, scientific, philosophising and poetical beings, resolute to carry the banner of 'Becoming' to unimaginable heights, is unquestionably the way forward.

CHAPTER 3

Clearing the Decks, Setting out our Stall and Introducing Life Chemistry.

Clearing the Decks. Our concern in this book consists of the effect of certain developments of the past 80 years on our human situation. In the previous two chapters we have presented a somewhat long summary of our human situation as it seemed to be in 1940 as a basis for appreciation and comparison with that of the present day. The temptation would then be to try to extrapolate for the next 80 years, taking us to 2100, but this would place too much strain on speculation, which would not be worthwhile, and so will be kept to a minimum. Accordingly, keeping the time range of the past 80 years in mind, we shall not consider the state of religions. We shall not deal with changes/developments in entropy theory, relativity theory, quantum mechanics, inflation theory, multiverses, black holes or dark matter, but we may deal briefly with electromagnetic fields. For all these interesting, if not fascinating topics that, for the most part, have not materially altered our situation, please refer to Cox and Cohen's recent and fine series of books about the Wonders of our solar-system, about our universe and about life itself. Analogously, we shall not deal with developments in robotics, potentially important as these are. As an introduction to this subject, please refer to Harari's compelling book entitled 'Sapiens, a Brief History of Humankind'.

Setting out our stall. To begin with, we shall introduce the chemistry of life, which, as we shall see, reinforces the physicists' conclusion that the universe, at an underlying level, is simple. After all, the whole of the matter (excluding dark matter) of life consists of chemistry. Then biochemistry and biology follow, and for us, then psychology, i.e. personality, and how, so far, we can determine this immaterial subject, in time and space.

Chemistry. There are 94 naturally occurring elements, the building blocks of all matter, in the universe. They are all composed of positive protons and neutral neutrons (in the nucleus) and external and equally charged, but negative, electrons. This is a huge simplification. They can be arranged in increasing order of the number of protons in their nuclei. These elements all derive from the simplest element, hydrogen, which contains only one proton as its nucleus, and one external electron, by fusion reactions occurring in various types of star, like our sun. The sun itself consists predominantly of hydrogen and helium (the second element) both in plasma form (i.e. stripped of electrons that whizz around) under these high temperature conditions. As the proton number in the nuclei of the atoms of each element increases, so the energy required to produce these by fusion increases. For example, the necessary energy to produce nuclei of elements with a higher number of protons than those of copper, is found in supernovae (see Cox and Cohen). For completeness, please note that there are two relatively stable 'isotopes' of hydrogen, called deuterium, and the mildly radioactive one, tritium. Their nuclei differ from that of hydrogen having one and two neutrons present there, as well as a proton, respectively. Similarly, many of the other 94 elements can exist as isotopes.

Digressing, just for a short time, we recall from the second chapter of our introductory, philosophical preamble, that we met the problem of 'the One' and 'the Many'. It was difficult to see how 'the One' could be transformed into 'the (very different) Many' of Leibniz and the Pluralists, and conversely how 'the Many' could have been produced without 'the One'. But if we look at our underlying, 'simple' universe, then we can see that 'the One' can be represented by hydrogen (as plasma, i.e. as protons, in stars) and that 'the Many' can be represented by all the naturally occurring elements (including hydrogen gas, as the first one) in the universe, which are responsible for all of its matter.

However, for all chemical reactivity purposes, it is only the electrons, or even the 'outer' electrons, which concern us; thus we no longer have to be concerned with <u>nuclei</u>. Our 94 elements can also be arranged, initially, and mostly, into 8 groups, in accordance with their physical and chemical properties, into the Periodic Table. The eighth group consists of a stable group of elements called the inert gases. All the other elements tend to react together to obtain the more stable, outer electron state of their most neighbouring inert gas in the Table. The first, two rows of the Periodic Table (presented below) contain many of the more prominent elements present in Life Chemical Compounds, i.e. Nitrogen(N); Hydrogen(H); Sulphur(S); Phosphorus(P); Sodium(Na); Calcium(Ca); Potassium(K) and Carbon(C). The letters in brackets are the chemical symbols for each specific element consisting of a single capital letter for the first letter of the element's name, followed, when necessary, by a characterising small letter, also from its name, to make the symbol specific. Some elements, which have been known for centuries, get their chemical symbols from their Latin names, thus the chemical symbol for Sodium(Na) comes from Natrium and that for Potassium(K), comes from Kalium. These chemical symbols provide a useful shorthand when writing the formulas for chemical compounds.

<u>The first two rows and two bits of the Periodic Table.</u>

Group 1   Group 8

H^1 He^2

Li^3 Be^4 B^5 C^6 N^7 O^8 F^9 Ne^{10}

Na^{11} Mg^{12} Al^{13} Si^{14} P^{15} S^{16} Cl^{17} Ar^{18}

K^{19} Ca^{20}

The superscript numbers show the numbers of protons in each element's nucleus. He stands for Helium; Li for Lithium; Be for Beryllium; B for Boron; F for Fluorine; Ne for Neon; Mg for Magnesium; Al for Aluminium; Si for Silicon; Cl for Chlorine and Ar for Argon.

<u>Life Chemical Compounds.</u> The element that enables the complexity of life is Carbon(C) [the element at the top of group 4 in the Table]. Carbon is unique because it can form so many life chemical compounds, not at all possible for any other element. Each different arrangement of atoms (a molecule) represents a different compound (composed of identical molecules) and each pure compound has its own characteristic set of chemical and physical properties. Organic Chemistry is the chemistry of carbon compounds and its basis depends upon its simple, structural theory. Over a million compounds of carbon are known today. Apart from life chemical compounds, organic chemistry covers the technologically important chemistry of, for example, dyes, drugs, paint, plastics, food, clothing, petrochemicals and rubber. A knowledge of organic chemistry is fundamental for students of medicine, and of the biological sciences.

<u>The Simple, Structural Theory of Carbon Compounds.</u> The 'covalent' bond results from the sharing of two electrons between elemental atoms, so that they approach, or obtain, the electron structure of a close inert gas. Typically, covalent bonds are used by carbon atoms to form their compounds. The simplest covalent bond is the one formed between two atoms of hydrogen to produce a hydrogen molecule, H_2.

$$H. + H. \rightarrow H:H$$

Each hydrogen atom has a single electron. By sharing it with another hydrogen atom, both atoms can mimic the stability of the electron state of the nearest inert gas, helium (electron structure 2) and so become more stable.

Similarly, methane is composed of 4 hydrogen atoms and one of carbon (electron structure 2,4). Since each carbon atom needs four extra electrons to obtain the stability of the inert gas neon (electron structure 2,8), sharing its electrons with 4 hydrogen atoms enables it to mimic the stability of the inert gas neon, whereas the four hydrogen atoms each now resemble the stability of the inert gas helium (electronic structure 2).

We say that carbon has a 'valency' of 4, whereas hydrogen has a 'valency' of 1. Note that a carbon atom could <u>lose</u> four electrons to obtain the stability of a helium atom but this would place 4 positive charges on the resulting carbon atom, which is an unstable situation electrostatically.

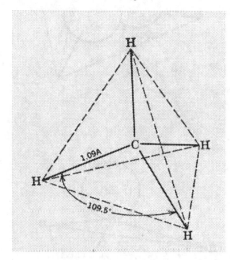

The covalent bonds already mentioned have length, strength and angles. Thus, a hydrogen molecule has a bond length of 0.74 Angstrom units (1 Angstrom unit (AU) = 10^{-8}m), and its strength is 103 kcals of energy. Here the angle of the bond is linear, or 180^0. For methane, each carbon hydrogen bond is 1.09 AU long; its strength is 101 kcals of energy and as all of the carbon hydrogen bonds are equivalent, as well as the most stable spatially, the angle between each H-C-H bond is the tetrahedral one of 109.5^0. Thus, carbon compounds mostly have

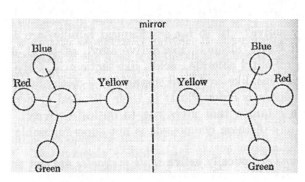

a three dimensional shape and as such are said to possess 'stereochemistry.'

Replacing all four of the hydrogen atoms attached to the carbon atom with 'functional' groups such as red, blue, yellow and green can lead to 'optical isomers' (mirror images) [see diagram] of tetrahedral structures. When all four groups bonded to the carbon atom are different, we produce two non-superimposable, [like our left and right hands] and so different, compounds. Interestingly, for life chemical compounds, only one of these 'optical isomers' is normally ever found.

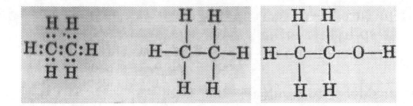

We can write structural formulas for organic compounds. For example, ethane, C_2H_6, and ethanol, C_2H_5OH, are as above.

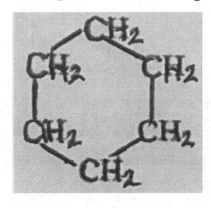

Cyclohexane, C_6H_{12}, can be written as shown left, but a more abbreviated form would be as shown right, in which the positions of the atoms of

carbon and hydrogen are assumed.

Structural formulas represent the various organic compounds, but they are not the compounds themselves – they are mental constructs of the compounds that help us to understand what they are like, but from these structures, even for very complicated ones, we can estimate accurately, and simply, what their physical and chemical properties will be. We can extend such structural formulas to compounds of other elements but these often involve 'ionic' (charged) bonds, such as for sodium chloride, Na^+Cl^-, in which the sodium atom has donated an electron to a chlorine atom, and so has become positively charged, and simultaneously, the chlorine atom has thereby become negatively charged. However, in this way, both atoms have obtained the stable electron states of their nearby inert gases. Sodium (electron structure 2,8,1) has become like Neon (2,8); and chlorine (2,8,7) has become like Argon (2,8,8). Generally, ionic bonds tend to be stronger than covalent ones; ionic compounds tend to be crystalline solids, but covalent ones tend to be waxy.

We can also improve our understanding of structural formulas visually by constructing three dimensional molecular models of them. For pure, crystalline compounds, we can use X-ray diffraction crystallography, as well as a scanning electron microscope. To identify unknown, pure compounds we can use elemental analysis to establish a molecular formula. We can identify the presence of 'functional' groups using infrared spectroscopy, and light absorbing structures by ultraviolet spectroscopy. Molecular weights can be found using a mass-spectrometer, and the structural positions of hydrogen atoms by nuclear magnetic resonance spectrometry. Most unknown compounds don't stay that way for long!

To continue, let us take a look at the following quotation:-

"Cabbages growing in the fields show a higher degree of chemical skill, than a higher race of beings exhibit in laboratories."

Now although the quotation is true, it is also a little unfair because the cabbages don't know that they are using chemical skill; it all happens involuntarily. We could modify the quotation by saying instead that:-

"Human beings involuntarily show a higher degree of chemical skill than they are capable of demonstrating in laboratories."

In other words, nature, through the passage of a billion years, probably carries out her chemistry more efficiently using enzymes as catalysts, than we can, consciously, in laboratories.

Vitamin B$_{12}$

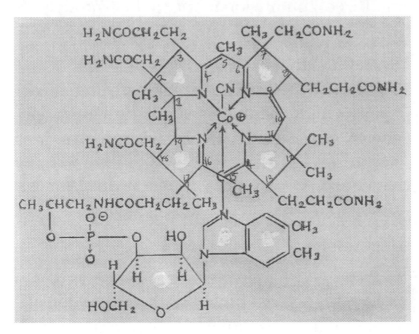

As an example, let us look briefly at vitamin B$_{12}$, effective in the cure of pernicious anaemia. In addition, the vitamin plays a key-role as a co-enzyme (i.e. that assists enzyme function) in normal brain activity; in the nervous system; in the formation of red blood cells, and is involved in the metabolism of every cell of the human body (especially in DNA synthesis) as well as in fatty- and amino-acid metabolism.

Vitamin B$_{12}$ is a water-soluble, dark red compound (this helps its purification by chromatography) with a presently accepted molecular formula of $C_{63}H_{90}CoN_{14}O_{14}$ containing at least 8 optically-active centres. Vitamin B$_{12}$ was the first life chemical compound known to contain the metallic element, Cobalt(Co). This metal atom is positioned in the centre of a tetrapyrrole (corrin, a 19 carbon atom ring, {see the diagram}) [c.f. haemaglobin has a 20 carbon atom ring]. Fascinatingly, neither fungi, plants, nor animals (including us) are capable of producing vitamin B$_{12}$ naturally. Only bacteria and archaea possess the enzymes necessary for its synthesis. Although the total, elegant, laboratory synthesis of vitamin B$_{12}$ was reported by R. B. Woodward (Nobel prize) during the 1960s, and by A. Eschenmoser in 1972, vitamin B$_{12}$ is produced industrially through a bacterial fermentation process.

Because bacteria and archaea are examples of single-celled procaryotes, it is tempting to suggest that the existence and viability of eucaryotes, and thence multicellular creatures, only became possible when the biochemistry of procaryotes had developed sufficiently (along with photosynthesis) some two billion years ago. As a result, it seems that eucaryotes lost the ability to generate their own vitamin B_{12}. Hence the prospects for really successful/useful chemotaxonomy (trying to trace the progress of evolution in plant families through the increasing complexity of their life chemical compounds) became poor probably because the required biochemistry had been established already, long before the onset of multicellular, biological evolution.

- -

CHAPTER 4

Personality - Derivation

"Know then thyself, presume not God to scan;
the proper study of mankind is Man."
An Essay on Man: Epistle II. Alexander Pope (1688 – 1744).

The Situation regarding DNA.

We can visualise the Earth as a (bio)sphere, covered with a thin skin of tissue called life. Living things are composed of invisible, soft, building blocks called cells, every one of which carries within itself the singular life chemical compound deoxyribonucleic acid (DNA). DNA is a large, life chemical compound with a complicated molecular formula made up from just five chemical elements, namely carbon,

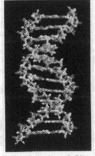

The structure of part of a DNA double helix

hydrogen, oxygen, nitrogen and phosphorus. In 1953, Crick and Watson resolved and reported the fundamental structure of DNA. It consists of two long strands along which genetic material (nucleotides A, C, G and T) is bonded regularly. In turn, this genetic material holds the strands together using hydrogen bonds, both tightly and loosely, as required. The strands run in opposite directions and are entwined like vines in the form of a double helix. Interestingly, solutions of left-handed, DNA double helices (as distinct from right-handed ones that contain more strain, and so tend not to exist) rotate the plane of polarised light

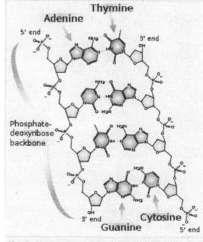

The chemical structure of DNA. Hydrogen bonds are shown as dotted lines.

to the left, suggesting an Earth-bound origin. How such a life chemical compound as complicated, and yet as simply efficient as

DNA, managed to evolve and replicate the way that it does and did, is a mystery with which our boggling minds struggle to get to grips.

DNA alone unites all life in a common history because every cell of every living thing has contained a version of DNA for a billion years. Because DNA can replicate itself, living things can produce offspring and so possess a common descent from shared ancestors. The breath-taking idea that a single DNA life form was the ancestor of all living things (called LUCA, i.e. the 'last universal common ancestor') spawns a sort of 'Big Birth' theory.

The growth of cells from a fertilised egg into a living creature is called development, and the development of life on Earth, is called evolution. Both development and evolution bring about structures of amazing complexity that are time-dependent and structured hierarchically, from the interaction of genes (entirely composed of DNA) with proteins.

The DNA in every cell of a person – called that person's genome – is very like an encyclopaedia in design and content. We ourselves, are very large compared to a cell, and cells are very large compared with the atoms of the chemical elements from which they, and so we, are made. We are composed of one hundred trillion (100 million, million, i.e. $10^2 \times 10^6 \times 10^6 = 10^{14}$) cells, and each cell is made up of one hundred trillion (10^{14}) atoms. Thus, the complexity of a cell in atomic terms, is about as great as the complexity of a person (brain included) in cellular terms.

The Situation regarding Astrology.

"The Name of the Game is Astrology,
The Name of the Game is DNA,
The Name of the Game is Life."
"For life, the Earth is the Centre of the Universe."

Addey has suggested, and recent results tend to confirm, that not only do we derive our physical form, but also our personalities, from our genes that have all become established, and essentially unchangeable, at our moment of fertilisation (Epoch). Despite our amazing ability to analyse DNA speedily into its fundamental genes, we are not capable of assigning immaterial, personality traits to particular genes. And even if we could, there still remains the problem of deciding how to interpret specifically what that personality trait is.

Natal astrology tells people about their individual personality traits, relationships, suitable careers and health. Thus, on the one hand, natal astrology resembles a behavioural, or social, science, but, on the other, the setting up of an astrological chart, centred on the Earth, is very much a part of a branch of physics (geocentric astronomy). Now the interpretation of our natal charts, cast for the times, dates and places of our moments of Epoch (fertilisation) and of Birth, describe our personalities, and we have seen that the likelihood is that we derive our character/personality from our genes. Potentially, these are two descriptions of the same thing, but, presently, the empirical, astrological descriptions of our character are much more readily accessible. Although we can conceive that planetary influences lie behind the origins of our personality genes, we may not be able to prove this to everyone's satisfaction.

Attempts to Prove the Truth of Natal Astrology.

Causation. Regardless of whether or not we are willing to classify Natal Astrology as a science, science and its methods currently play an important rôle in trying to establish its truth. However, budding astrologers, having interpreted the natal charts of their family and friends, have little difficulty in accepting it. But many people can't imagine how natal astrology can possibly work. They require answers to questions such as, "How on Earth can the planet Venus impart differing, harmonising characteristics to different people's person-alities depending simply on the time when, and the place where, they were born?" To try to answer this deceptively simple, yet extremely difficult question, let us examine some of the physical evidence:

1) Roberts has pointed out that planetary influences must travel at the speed of light.

2) If the cosmic bodies are ranked in order of possible causative forces, then there is no correlation with tidal forces, with mass displacement and with brightness. The only other factor capable of avoiding incompatibilities in these three, is resonance.

3) ELF (electrostatic life fields) consisting of waves between 3 -> 300 Hz (and possibly VLF waves of up to 10,000 Hz) are of interest. These are the frequency ranges of the electromagnetic fields of living organisms, and of many natural, geophysical phenomena. [Apparently, solar radiation of frequencies lower than 20,000 Hz cannot reach the Earth]. Yet ELF waves are almost impossible to stop due to their large wavelength (about 10^5 km for 1 ->10 Hz) waves. On the other hand, a strong resonant action with fundamental, biological fields may occur. There is evidence that living organisms, like ourselves, respond to ELF waves by affecting our reaction response times.

4) Tomaschek has stated that there are, beyond doubt, correlations between the positions and angles (e.g. 0, 30, 45, 60, 90, 120, 135, 150 and 180^0) subtended at the Earth (at the Eastern Horizon and/or at the middle of the sky) by two planets, with terrestrial events. He listed four possibilities for explaining such correlations:

   a) Celestial bodies actually OPERATE upon terrestrial events.
   b) Celestial bodies PRECIPITATE such events.
   c) Celestial bodies SYNCHRONISE with such events, and
   d) Celestial bodies SYMBOLISE organic cosmic forces.

Possibility a) is unlikely due to the small energies (e.g. from gravitational forces) involved. Roberts has strongly and adversely criticised possibility c) and possibility d) could prove to be a higher order extension of possibility b). As a result, we shall concentrate our thoughts and efforts on possibility b). Here, like possibility a), energy is involved, but it is a minimum value required for initiation. This then is hugely magnified by resonance and given the necessary selection, or variation, depending on the frequencies involved.

<u>Astrological Causation and Resonance.</u> Resonance has become an essential consideration in any theory of astrological causation. However, until more is known about causation forces (electromagnetic influences?) the following discussion has to remain purely speculative and should be taken only as illustrative of the concept.

Unless a body generates a frequency of some kind that can interact with the frequencies of other bodies to give a resonance peak, then it will remain ineffective. For example, the stars do not swamp mass displacement effects because they show negligible, apparent motion, and so do not generate a suitable frequency. Also, a planet's frequency may well vary according to certain factors, such as the eccentricity of its orbit, hence it may resonate better at certain times rather than at others. In other words, astrology may work only some of the time.

Collin has suggested that the planets move around the Sun at varying distances from it, roughly in circular orbits. But the Sun is also moving (slowly) in a much vaster orbit around the black hole at the centre of our Milky Way galaxy, carrying the whole of its solar system with it. If we go back and try to visualise the continuous movement of the solar system in space, then we can build a picture of a central glowing filament (the path of the Sun) surrounded by a number of coils at different distances, and of various conducting planets (or of various planetary electromagnetic fields) within the Sun's electromagnetic heliosphere. An electrician would recognise such a picture as a representation of a poly-phase transformer (transponder), presumably constructed for the purpose of stepping down the solar energy in several different ratios and transmitting it to us (on Earth).

Thus, it can be postulated that the planets modulate the Sun continuously, and that the modulated solar radiation is transformed to a biologically active frequency *via* excitation of the Earth – ionosphere cavity. That is, the planets set the scene, and the Sun provides the power. Such a theory would be compatible with the findings of Nelson and Fox, with the known characteristics of ELF waves, and with astrological tradition. But to derive a more plausible model, we must examine certain fundamental considerations about resonance and cycles, which, up to now, seem to have been overlooked.

Planets and Solar Cycles.

The phenomena of latitude passage in solar cycles (i.e. sunspots) shows that 1) aspects are not the primary causation factor because an aspect cannot act at different places at different times, and 2) the causative factor must synchronise with the solar equator because sunspot formation is symmetrical about it. Thus, the key question is, "What planetary factor synchronises with the solar equator, in tune with the solar cycle of sunspots?" The duration of the major sunspot cycle is 22.2 years. The Jupiter/Neptune (JU/NE) cycle is 22.13 years, shows excellent timing and negligible drift and so it is reasonable to assume that the major controlling factor (along with several other factors) of the sunspot solar cycle is indeed the JU/NE one. The dominance of the JU/NE cycle is due to three factors:-

1) Resonance. This is the main reason.
2) The uniformity of Neptune's orbit that helps to maintain synchronisity, and
3) The large mass of the planets involved. Jupiter and Neptune rank first and third respectively in terms of Mass Displacement.

Minima (in sunspot activity) can be explained by considering Neptune – Pluto resonances linked, once again, to the solar equator. (Any trans-Plutonium planet (e.g. Sedna?) may have a significant long-term effect on the wave-envelope of sunspot number).

The Sun is spinning like a gyroscope, and so resists changes in tilt. But the entire solar system is also spinning like a gyroscope, except that the weights, and hence the tilt, are being shifted continuously. Hence there are two gyroscopes working against each other: one fixed (the Sun), and the other moving (the solar system). Thus, the Sun is being nudged continuously, and the result is a continuous cycle of disturbance. The results obtained are consistent with variations in angular momentum. The relatively tiny mass of all the planets compared with the Sun, is offset by their containing 98% of the angular momentum.

Planets and Terrestrial Cycles.

The same model as applied to the Sun can also be applied to the Earth. Seymour, while acknowledging that the planetary influences (gravitational/electromagnetic) are weak, claims that planetary gravitational pull on the Earth's upper atmosphere (just like the Moon's gravity helps to generate the tides on Earth) while extremely weak, can undergo huge (10,000 x) resonance amplification that, in turn, disturbs Earth's magnetic field (just like the Moon can).

Seymour claims that his theory can predict the relative variations of the planetary influences, from their point of closest approach to the Earth, compared with that when they are furthest away. Also, he claims that his theory can explain the observed effects for geomagnetically disturbed days.

Where the rotating Earth replaces the rotating Sun, the angle between the ecliptic and the Earth's equator is $23\frac{1}{2}^0$ (c.f. for the Sun, the equator makes an angle of $7\frac{1}{4}^0$ with the ecliptic). The planetary effect on Earth should start at a latitude four times higher, i.e. roughly at the poles, and should reach the equator 0.5 cycle (observed is 0.7 cycle) later (c.f. the Sun, for which sunspot formation moves from + or − 30⁰ of solar latitude, i.e. four times the angle of the solar equator with the ecliptic).

It then follows that all cycles that manifest on the Sun should also be found on Earth (however, if the terrestrial response is insensitive to phase, then all terrestrial periods will tend to be half the relevant solar ones). The important point is that the model implies that planets affect the Earth directly, and not *via* the Sun.

These findings 1) provide a basis for a plausible model of astrological causation. They may 2) lead to an understanding of how aspects work, and why rising planets are significant. In general, the findings may well give dramatic insight into the workings of astrological causation.

Possible intermediate stages.

Collin states that it is possible to show that the situation of the main centres of man's physical system bear the same relationship to each other as the planets of the solar system do. Each glandular centre (e.g. the gonads, the pituitary and the pineal glands) therefore is a receiving station for one particular form of solar energy transmitted by the transforming agency of the corresponding planet in the solar system. Thus, the resulting geomagnetic disturbances of the appropriate frequencies, then influence our nervous system, and, in turn, our relevant glands.

Taking an indirect line, Seymour proposes that the fluctuations in the Earth's magnetic field, can cause impulses to pass along our nerve cells that, in turn, are detected by our central nervous system, in a way similar to that of how a T.V. aerial + tuned receiver, picks up radio waves.

Alternatively, Roberts has proposed that an intangible, flower-like organ, senses the magnetic disturbances in the form of psychic waves that somehow become manifested as our personality characteristics.

For completeness, magnetic disturbances can alter rotations of plane polarised light. Perhaps it is these that we detect with our eyes, presumably in an involuntary fashion.

After Birth – Proof.
The Gauquelins' Work on élite Professionals – Sports Champions and the Mars Effect.

Astrologically, the interpretation of the planet Mars in natal charts involves words such as heat, energy and initiatory force. As a result, we could expect that the planet Mars will feature strongly in the natal charts of sports champions. Using statistical methods, the Gauquelins rigorously and objectively detected a Mars Effect in the birth charts of sports champions, which Ertel confirmed. However, they devised their own system of sector distributions in order to observe the Mars Effect without statistical bias (but also without astrological logic). But the simple, Morinus House System that has world-wide applicability, has its own specific Ascendant, the Morin Point, which is not too far removed from the 'Oblique Ascension' used by the Gauquelins.

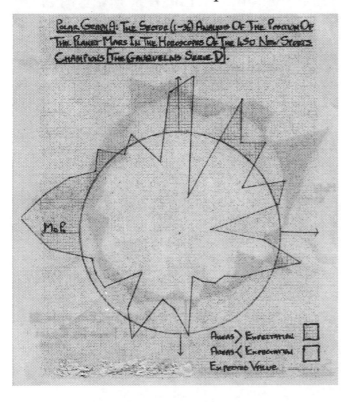

Accordingly, Graph A shows the equal sector positions (1 ->36), counting from the Morin Point, of the planet Mars, in the Morinus birth charts of the 450 New Sports Champions File (Serie D). The outer circle gives the average number expected (12.5) for a uniform distribution. Areas greater than expected were found clustered around the Morin Point particularly, but also near to the Morinus 'midheaven' (the middle of the sky above). Notice that there are substantially greater Mars sector occupancies above the Morin Point (253) than those below it (197) suggesting that sports champions tend to have Mars positioned above the Earth at birth, and so will tend to be more objective regarding sports affairs than generally. Similarly, there are greater Mars sector occupancies to the East (left) side of the chart, rather than in those on the West (right).This indicates that the sport destiny of the champions lies mainly in their own hands, rather than depending on others, or on circumstances. These reasonable results indicate a different, independent type of proof for the truth of natal astrology.

After Birth – Proof. Conquerors of the World.

Here we are asking, "What is the main astrological indicator common to conquerors (1st Tier, Power Notables) of the World?" There are three main indicators for interpretation of any natal chart; these are the positions of the Sun, of the Moon and of the Morin Point. Traditionally, we have determined astrological character by interpreting the indicators present in our Birth charts. But now we shall recommend that it should be based, substantially, on our Epoch charts as well.

The first assumption made, is that we can use interpretations of indicators for the Epoch chart in just the same way, and just as well, as we can normally for the Birth chart. Secondly, we shall assume that interpretations for the Epoch chart will have equal weighting with those of the Birth chart. The rules of 'The Pre-Natal Epoch' clearly specify the relationships between the Morin Points and the positions of the Moon, both at Epoch and at Birth. Table 1 assembles the data for the three main indicators for the natal charts of six, 1st tier, power notables (our conquerors of the World) [see the author's, "When Scorpio Ruled the World"].

Table 1: The Sign Decanates containing the Sun, Moon and Morin Point for the Epoch and Birth Charts of the Six Power Notables.

Name	<-- Epoch --> Sun	Moon	MoPo	<-- Birth --> Sun	Moon	MoPo
Edward III	1st Aquarius	3rd Taurus	1st Scorpio	3rd Scorpio	1st Taurus	3rd Scorpio
A Hitler	3rd Leo	1st Scorpio	1st Capricorn	1st Taurus	1st Capricorn	1st Scorpio
J Stalin	1st Pisces	1st Scorpio	1st Aries	3rd Sagittarius	1st Libra	1st Scorpio
Napoleon	1st Scorpio	3rd Aries	3rd Cancer	3rd Leo	3rd Capricorn	3rd Libra
J Caesar	3rd Libra	1st Aries	1st Scorpio	3rd Cancer	1st Scorpio	1st Aries
Alexander the Great	1st Scorpio	2nd Pisces	1st Sagittarius	3rd Cancer	1st Sagittarius	2nd Pisces

Table 1 shows that the 1st decanate (1 of 36 for the complete Zodiac) of Scorpio occurs more often than any of the others. This is our indicator common to conquerors. All six notables have at least one entry, and Hitler, Stalin and Caesar have two, even though these occur because the Order of their Epoch requires this. Words that describe traits of the 1st Scorpio decanate indicator include prudent, self-controlled and highly dignified, as well as penetrative, mystical and intelligent. Speculatively, yet interestingly, our present Queen, Elizabeth II, has the first decanate of Scorpio at her Morin Point at Birth.

After Birth – Proof.

Comparisons of Royal, Astrological, Character Portraits with Independent, Individual Biographies.

There are two major advantages of using England's rulers for constructing astrological, character portraits. Firstly, for centuries past, their birth times, dates and places have been recorded carefully. Secondly, all the rulers have had their biographies written, although perhaps, not completely without bias. Nevertheless, we are able to use them to form a considered opinion of the character portraits produced.

The character portraits were constructed using the author's proposed method of combining interpretations from individual Epoch and Birth charts (see 'Heaven's Message'). None of the interpretations were his, but were taken from those described in books by notable astrologers that had no connection whatsoever with the rulers concerned. The assembled interpretations were sorted and blended into what was hoped would be a readily understandable whole. All points in the interpretations were included but duplication was minimised. Importantly, the unpolished portraits were impartial, consisting of relatively modern expressions for appreciation and for comparison with each one's biography. Several royal families were met, from the Plantagenet kings to the Saxe-Coburg and Gotha monarchs. Also, by treating each family separately as a group, attempts were made to try to find internal group hereditary characteristics among the members of each family.

We could conclude that all the character portraits of the rulers fitted them well, thereby adding another independent type of support for the truth of natal astrology. Because of all the foregoing evidence in this chapter, the author is tempted to conclude that character portraits should be able to provide all of us with guidance, firstly as young adults and secondly as parents, soon after a child is born, but here, using the child's own character portrait.

Let us now try to combine the foregoing physical evidence for astrological involvement with the detection side plus the biological side (see the author's books, "Our Birth on Earth" and "Heaven's Message"). Additionally, we shall try to incorporate it all into the genetic description of our Birth process as well as with the rules of the Pre-Natal Epoch.

Let us assume for simplicity that the planetary, electromagnetic, resonant influences impinge directly on the Earth. Also, let us assume that the detection method consists of the intangible, flower-like organ, which passes the information to the brain, which, in turn, transfers it to the hormone supplying endocrine glands that trigger the testes and the ovaries. Thus, the monthly pre-selected egg, containing built-in characteristics of its time, combines with the single selected sperm, also containing a matching set of characteristics for its time, resulting in the fertilised egg. Hence, at this moment of fertilisation (the Epoch) there is a combination of the mother's timely appropriate genes along with an equal set of timely, appropriate genes from the father. (Notice that the characteristics of time, supplied at the Epoch, also contain within them the characteristics required for the time of Birth!) Additionally, at this moment (the Epoch) the sex of the baby is determined by the sex chromosome from the father.

Now the Moon regulates the child's involuntary development in the womb following the rules of the Pre-Natal Epoch, through the flower-like organ and *via* the pituitary and hypothalamus glands, thereby triggering the placenta to regulate pregnancy. Hence, the Birth occurs (with the involvement of the foetus) at the pre-arranged time. Broadly speaking, in this way, we suggest that nature miraculously achieves the birth of a child, furnished with the characteristics of its time (i.e. its personality, its heredity traits, as well as its physical form).

- -

CHAPTER 5

Personality – Producing a Character Portrait

"No-one can make the fullest use of his/her opportunities, material or spiritual, in this World, without a close and deep study of his/her nativity."
A. Leo, *Astrology for All.*

The desire for greater understanding and awareness of how human beings fit into the scheme of things within our star (solar) system ensures Astrology's survival in the World. Because change and upheaval continue to disrupt our culture due to natural disasters, wars, social/political revolution, mental and physical illness, nervous disorders and accidents, Astrology is able to provide us with a strong base of pattern, rhythm and order that otherwise is noticeably missing. One reason behind the existence of this strong base lies in the essentially constant variety of human nature throughout written history. Probably, in no previous age, has such a strong base been more important and so badly needed.

Contrary to public perception, modern astrologers are wary of predicting events. They believe that Astrology's greatest practical value lies in the diagnosis of a person's character coupled with the assessment of his/her potential. Having assembled a person's characteristics, we can pick out his/her strengths and weaknesses and so try to decide what suits him/her best. Armed with the unbiased insight into his/her qualities of disposition and temperament that they find themselves endowed with, the belief is that they can lead better, happier and more fulfilled, purposeful lives through this enhanced understanding of themselves.

One great difficulty for Astrology is specifying interpretations accurately enough, especially when compared with that of specifying the contents of natal charts. As the accuracy of character interpretations is much broader (because they are abstract) they could become improved with greater experience of working with natal charts coupled then with greater confidence in their correctness. Hone and Mayo recommended the use of keywords that tended to reduce an astrologer's subjectivity at an early stage and placed significant emphasis on preparation for interpretation. All this involved considerable time and effort, producing a stilted character assessment that then required converting into acceptable English.

A possible, alternative method uses interpretations of indicators published by eminent astrologers, based on their hard work, built-up experience and special aptitude, together with logical deduction and good practice. Blending their interpretations into an acceptable result also takes time and effort and produces a stilted result but it has the virtues of objectivity and impartiality. On balance, we have used this method.

Traditionally, we derived astrological character by interpreting the indicators present in the birth chart alone. But now we recommend the use of the Epoch chart to the same extent as well, for this purpose. There are three main indicators for interpretation for both Epoch and Birth charts. These comprise the position of the Sun, of the Moon and of the Morin Point. We could use a full-blown set of indicators but, more practically, we can generate a relevant character portrait that will cover the more important characteristics of a person, which should suffice for our purpose. Experience teaches that the indicators that we shall use for assembling a character portrait from both Epoch and Birth (Natal) charts consist of:

1) Planetary Distribution and Overall Chart Shape.
2) Specific Interplanetary Aspect Patterns.
3) Sun and Moon sign combination.
4) Sun and Moon House combination.
5) Strongest Aspects only to the Sun and Moon.
6) Morin Point by sign and decanate.

7) Chart and decanate rulers by sign, House and the strongest aspects they receive.

8) Rising planets and Retrograde Personal planets.

9) Remaining personal planets, i.e. any; or all of Mercury, Venus and Mars, by sign, House and the strongest aspects separately that they receive.

The ways in which these indicators provide us with interpretations has been given fully in the author's "Heaven's Message", Ch. 6.

Books used by the author to provide relevant interpretations include:

1) "How to learn Astrology" and "A Guide to Horoscope Interpretation" by M. E. Jones.

2) "Astrology for All" and "How to Judge a Nativity" by A. Leo.

3) "The Modern Textbook of Astrology" by M. E. Hone.

4) "Astrology: How to Cast Your Horoscope" by R. C. Davison.

5) "Planets in Houses" by R. Pelletier.

6) "The Cosmic Influence" by F. X. King.

7) "Karmic Astrology – Retrogrades and Reincarnation" by M. Schulman.

Additionally, the assembly of the interpretations into four main groups, namely character, relationships, career and health, and the ways in which these are subdivided, blended and ordered into an understandable whole, has been presented in Ch. 7, Ch. 8, Ch. 9 and Ch. 10 of the author's "Heaven's Message".

The finished horoscope, containing the person's charts and the deliberately unpolished character portrait, is then introduced (see "Heaven's Message", p 94 and p 126) by the following:

Dear Person,

<u>Heaven's Message.</u>

Most people know that the signs of the Zodiac are the familiar part of Astrology. Newspapers and magazines emphasise that sign containing the Sun, since we can all know our own sign from our individual dates of birth. However, serious astrologers know that the sign ascending over the Horizon is at least as equal importance. But this ascending sign, at the Morin Point, can only be found when the moment of birth is known, and is therefore specific for the person for whom the chart is drawn up. In a related way that the Sun is an important planet for men, so the Moon is an important planet for women, although both are important for both sexes.

Actually, there are two moments, that of Birth and that of Fertilisation (the Epoch), which are important astrologically. In all probability, we derive our characteristics from our genes that became established at our 'Moment of Fertilisation'. Perhaps this Epoch time shows the inherent character of the new person soon to become manifest in the flesh, whereas the Birth time may denote the actual, personal conditions into which the new person is born. We combine the interpretations from the Epoch and Birth charts to generate "Heaven's Message" for the person under consideration. Please note that none of the interpretation is mine; I have simply taken the interpretations of the various indicators from standard text-books, and have tried to blend them into a readily understandable whole.

Specifically, your own Birth chart shows that:

The sign containing the Morin Point is Capricorn,
The sign containing the Moon is Aquarius and
The sign containing the Sun is Cancer.

Similarly, your own Epoch chart shows that:

The sign containing the Morin Point is Aquarius,
The sign containing the Moon is Capricorn and
The sign containing the Sun is Scorpio.

Hence, your character contains much that is a mixture of the traits associated with Capricorn, Aquarius, Cancer and Scorpio.

Probably, it is best that you yourself should not judge the interpretation, but rather let someone who knows you well judge it with you. Basically, "Heaven's Message" attempts to supply the requirements for satisfying the old Greek dictum, "Man, know thyself" (presumably both individually and collectively).

The general idea is for <u>you</u> to decide what suits <u>you</u> best; to build on <u>your</u> strengths; to guard against <u>your</u> weaknesses and to reinforce your own personal judgement. In this way, <u>your</u> "Heaven's Message" tries to be useful.

Concerning this whole chapter, it would be extremely useful if a computer program could be produced that would combine all the contents of this chapter and so generate "Heaven's Message" quickly and efficiently. The time and trouble saved by astrologers would be considerable indeed.

CHAPTER 6

Our Simple, Present (2020 A.D.) Situation

In chapters 1 and 2 we read about general descriptions of parts of our 1940 A.D. situation. Most of these still seem applicable and relevant now, eighty years later.

<u>General Points.</u>

The very particular chemical properties of the elements oxygen, hydrogen and carbon made a habitable World possible. This happened because the reactions between these elements, as revealed by their positions in the Periodic Table, explain the overall composition of the World, and help us to determine how, and whether or not, they will react with other elements there.

These days, we can 'see' genes using a scanning electron microscope. These genes lead to 'bundles' of inherited, genetic characteristics from within our various chromosomes. This idea of 'bundles' of characteristics, making up our personalities, fits so well with astrological descriptions of our being. The 'planets' of the Earth each have their own principles, e.g. the Sun stands for power, will, vitality and self-expression, which collected together, for each individual, form a 'bundle' of personality traits. We have proposed that each person has two such bundles that are derived from the situation of the solar system, with respect to the Earth, at each person's time, date and place of Birth, as well as at each one's time, date and place of Epoch/fertilisation. In this way, each person has his/her own characteristics of his/her time that are fixed in place no later than when his/her birth process is complete. How flexible these genes, or characteristics, are, is open to question, but it does call into doubt the application of brain-washing techniques to try to improve, or change, a person's character significantly. Each individual, unique person is the emergent result of that person's characteristics of his/her two times, his/her physical form, as well as traits from his/her family heredity. This combination provides each one of us with something personal, but not ungiven. If this paragraph is largely correct, then we can dispense with the proposal that we select our present situation from a previous one. The genetic mechanism of our birth process explains how 'I' should be here and in this region of time.

One challenge for our brains is to try to justify our selfishness and direct it to our advantage, but we must guard against praying for deliverance from our problems, and then turn our backs on the ambitions and pursuits of contending nations.

Turning now to the eye, as one of our evolved organs, it has been proposed that ancient cyanobacteria, possibly by chance, produced a common form of light sensitive rhodopsin. Both vertebrates and invertebrates used this as the starting point for the evolution of their eyes (see Cox and Cohen in 'Wonders of Life' p 213).

We grow old, stiffen and die because the constituents of our bodies decay over time from interactions with disease, malnutrition, oxygen of the air and cosmic rays. Preventing, healing and controlling such as these should enable us to increase our life expectancies, which, now, are approximately the double of those of 1940. Recently, a life-expectancy of 125 years has been suggested as a maximum for human beings. However, when the brain dies, and so loses its complexity, so consciousness and its memories are lost also.

A perfect World has never existed. The suggestion is that nature undertook it to try to develop more consciousness through evolution, for our universe. Consciousness comes with us, and with others around, before and after, us, but for each of us, to start with, the brain is a blank slate that only starts to learn about the World from its senses, from birth onwards. Possibly, consciousness of a different kind from ours, may emerge from inorganic complex life within, e.g. a supercomputer.

Organisms, including ourselves, behave as though they had an end in view. This internal teleology of individual beings can be rationalised as part of the trend towards increased consciousness. In the author's 'Our Birth on Earth', we met Teilhard de Chardin's extension of Darwin's work. Teilhard (1881 – 1955) proposed that the motivation for evolution in our World/universe is the striving towards increased consciousness. This can be achieved in four ways:

1) By increasing the numbers of life of a particular kind (probably leading to over-population, starvation and migration).

2) By increasing the life-expectancy of a particular kind (the resultant striving for longer life-expectancy may constitute one reason why migrations of people occur, i.e. looking for a better life to live longer).

3) By evolving more conscious life from conscious forms already present. The most versatile and viable form of life on Earth is ourselves, i.e. homo-sapiens. The question arises, "Can we wait for nature to produce (long-term), or make ourselves into (short-term) more conscious/intelligent forms?" However, there will be biological as well as ethical problems associated with this.

4) By creating more conscious, inorganic life-forms by intelligent design (see Harari, "Sapiens", Ch, 20, and Cox and Cohen, "Human Universe", p 142) at least as complex as the human brain. But what sort of sentience will emerge?

Several points and questions arose in Chapters 1 and 2, which we can try to answer now:-

1) To the question, "Why should we try to transcend life?" We can answer, "Because this is the path to a better life, increased possibilities and greater consciousness."

2) To the question, "What is our task?" We can answer, "We must try to increase consciousness throughout our World/universe."

This implies that life on Earth, and mankind in particular, are extremely important due to the large contribution they make to the consciousness of our universe. This seems to be a commodity that is in extremely short supply throughout it.

3) We can ask, "What does human experience tell us?" And we can answer, "Its meaning tells us how to build on what we know already."

4) Again, we can ask, "How came this strange experience to be ours?" and again, we could answer, "Because the Earth/Moon system is the only stable place in our solar system, if not in our Milky Way galaxy, where intelligent life can develop and be supported."

5) To the question, "What is the meaning and purpose of experience, if it have any?" To which we can reply, "From its meaning we can plan for our future and its purpose is to achieve the future and so generate for us more new and better opportunities."

6) The answer to the questions, "What is truth?" "What is beauty?" and "What is goodness?" will be unacceptable on the grounds that qualities such as these are bound to be too subjective.

7) But we can also ask, "How can the insubstantial, i.e. Space and Time, come into contact with, or have any relation with, the substantial objects around us?" and also, "How came material things to enter this immaterial substance?" The answer here could involve 'spontaneous symmetry breaking' by cooling from very high temperatures (see Cox and Cohen, Wonders of the Universe, pp 102 – 106).

8) Similarly, "How can thought lay hold on substance?" Can anyone explain how the basically simple harmony between thought and things came about? It seems as if nature had been arranged expressly to suit our purposes of comprehension.

Conclusions:

From Teilhard de Chardin: Evolution proceeds by development of mind/spirit through the increased complexity of matter, rather than through Darwinian "survival of the fittest". It is the process of groping blindly, combined with the two-fold mechanisms of reproduction and heredity (as the hoarding and additive improvement of favourable conditions obtained, without the diminution, indeed with the increase, of the number of individuals engaged), which gives rise to the extraordinary assemblage of living stems forming the tree of life. In animals, consciousness shows itself instinctively but humans, uniquely, have gone a stage further in that they can think well constructively. Individuals collectively contribute to the noosphere, the Earth's consciousness, as the next superior layer to the biosphere. Further rises of consciousness will come as mankind manages to unify itself into ever more complicated societies/ arrangements leading finally to the 'Omega' point.

These days, we seem to be close to possessing eternal youth along with the powers of creation and destruction. Much has been achieved, but, possibly as a result, many other animals are approaching extinction. We still don't know how to direct ourselves and so tend to behave irresponsibly.

Selfishly, anarchy rules, but there seems to be no lasting satisfaction. When we don't know what we truly want, then are situation becomes dangerous (see Harari, Ch. 20).

To our knowledge, we humans are the most conscious, aware beings in our universe. But to our short-term, cramped existence, there seems to be no genuine worth. However, there is meaning to our universe, because of our continual existence through reproduction. Our society is the most complicated, improving system within it. Our chances of being here, after four billion years of life on Earth, have been remote indeed, but this rarity makes us extremely valuable.

Our foremost aim is to guarantee that one human society must always survive, and this must take precedence over any other considerations that we may have. This is absolutely primary.

For the near future: firstly, this means developing a comprehensive detecting system for asteroids potentially on track to collide with the Earth. Secondly, we must establish what we all need to do, should we detect any such asteroid (see Cox and Cohen, 'Human Universe' p 234).

From MacNeile Dixon: How simple then, is our duty – loyalty to life, to the ship's company and to ourselves, so that it may not be through our surrender that the great experiment of existence, whose issue remains in doubt, can come to an end in nothingness. "We must not obey," said Aristotle, "those who urge us, because we are human and mortal, to think only human and mortal thoughts; in so far as we may, we should practise immortality, and to omit no effort to live, in accordance, with the best that is in us." We should think that this singular race of indomitable, scientific, philosophising and poetical beings, resolute to carry the banner of 'Becoming' to unimaginable heights, is unquestionably the way forward.

- -

Printed in the United States
By Bookmasters